Offshore ADVANTAGE

Offshore ADVANTAGE

A Canadian Guide to Wealth Creation, Asset Protection & Estate Planning

GORDON LAIGHT

Canadian Cataloguing in Publication Data

Laight, Gordon
Offshore advantage

Includes index.
ISBN 0-13-929498-8

1. Investments, Canadian. 2. Tax havens. 3. Finance, Personal. I. Title

HG4538.L8 1998 332.6'042 C98-932068-5

Prentice-Hall Canada Inc., Scarborough, Ontario
A Division of Simon & Schuster/A Viacom Company

Prentice-Hall, Inc., Upper Saddle River, New Jersey
Prentice-Hall International (UK) Limited, London
Prentice-Hall of Australia, Pty. Limited, Sydney
Prentice-Hall Hispanoamericana, S.A., Mexico City
Prentice-Hall of India Private Limited, New Delhi
Prentice-Hall of Japan, Inc., Tokyo
Simon & Schuster Southeast Asia Private Limited, Singapore
Editora Prentice-Hall do Brasil, Ltda., Rio de Janeiro

ISBN 0-13-929498-8

Director, Trade Group: Robert Harris
Consulting Editor: Brian Noble, Financial Communications
Copy Editor: Rodney Rawlings
Assistant Editor: Joan Whitman
Production Editor: Lu Cormier
Production Coordinator: Shannon Potts
Art Direction: Mary Opper
Cover Design: Gary Beelik
Cover Photograph: Ken Davies, Masterfile
Page Layout: Richard Hunt, Archetype

1 2 3 4 5 RRD 02 01 00 99 98

Printed and bound in the United States of America

table of CONTENTS

Acknowledgments

As I look back on the time and energy it has taken to research and write this book, I have to think about the many people who have crossed my path in life — the mentors, teachers, colleagues and friends who imparted the knowledge, provided the insights and peeled back the layers of what is, in my opinion, the most compelling industry in the world: international investment, banking and finance. Offshore is essentially a component of this industry, albeit an important one, and its relevance will continue to grow, thanks in large part to the many people whose assistance made this book a reality.

The person I want to thank first and foremost is Brian Noble of Financial Communications in Toronto. Brian has been the guiding force behind this project, and his editorial and financial skills have been a tremendous help to me in writing this book, as was his ability to keep me from becoming distracted. His influence can be felt throughout its pages. On a further editorial note, both Brian and I benefited enormously from the professionalism and commitment of Robert Harris and his Prentice Hall team.

One person I cannot thank enough is Charles Cain, Chairman of Skye Fiduciary Services on the Isle of Man and editor of the magazine *Offshore Investment.* He and Professor Peter Willoughby of Deacon Graham & James Hong, were instrumental in providing some of the most interesting and relevant information on offshore in general, as well as on company and trust structures. I first met Mr. Cain and Professor Willoughby at the annual conference sponsored by *Offshore Investment* at Jesus College, Oxford, in September 1997. This conference is a wonderful experience for anyone in the offshore industry at any level because of the incredible amount of information that is imparted by a great many of the industry's leading minds.

I would especially like to thank Brian Stammer, who, as editor and publisher of *Offshore Finance Canada,* gave me both the opportunity and support to become a regular contributor to his unique and informative publication. My regular contributions were the impetus behind this book.

I would also like to thank Robert Milroy, who is editor of a wonderful publication entitled *The Micropal Guide to Offshore Investment Funds,* for allowing me to use some of the incredibly informative material contained within its pages. This publication is a valuable resource for anyone looking for offshore funds.

I thank Hywel Jones, Managing Director of the Britannia Consulting Group in Nassau, for his contributions of mirth, perceptiveness and intelligence to the lives of both my wife and myself in our new home. I also thank him along with Peter Fletcher and Mike Azad for their contributions to the section on Bahamian limited partnerships. Offshore limited partnerships and offshore foundations will continue to rise in prominence as replacements for the ailing trust vehicles of yesteryear, and these gentlemen have the skills and knowledge to assist anyone who is examining the multitude of offshore opportunities.

Thanks to Robert Hindle of Hindle and Associates for his assistance and guidance on all things taxable, as well as for his contributions of information and insight to this project. My gratitude is also expressed to Garry Duncan of BDO Dunwoody for his assistance on tax and non-residency issues based on his publication *Canadian Residents Abroad.* I thank Messrs. Michael Paton, Brian Simms and David Johnstone, partners of the firm Lennox Paton, for their guidance and wisdom of the many laws and legislative initiatives that make The Bahamas the jurisdiction that it is, as well as for their valuable contributions to the process. And a hearty thank you to John Perry Bujouves, Executive Vice President of Globacor Consultants Corporation, whose expertise helped tremendously in providing a well-rounded conclusion and further commentary.

Also, I thank John Xanthoudakis, Chairman of the Norshield Financial Group, who provided both my wife and me with the opportunity to explore the offshore world and learn many of the nuances that make this industry what it is.

Most importantly, I thank my wife, Donna, without whose love, unwavering support, ability, acumen and insight, my life would be far less than what it is.

Gordon Laight

Introduction

If you're glancing through this book in your local bookstore, trying to ferret out the latest and slickest techniques for getting your loot offshore—this isn't it. How-to books in the areas of finance, taxation and investing become stale too quickly as the overall environment, governmental regulations and individual circumstances change so quickly.

Offshore is not a new concept. But you wouldn't necessarily know that from the media, where it has been garnering quite a lot of attention over the recent past. Witness the Airbus scandal (or lack thereof) and its focus on Switzerland and Luxembourg. Or the issue of the looted Jewish gold, the Holocaust and the Swiss banks. And every Canadian's once-favourite stock, Bre-X Minerals, which has turned into an offshore saga as more and more attention is being focused on the former principals and their offshore lifestyles.

Part of this recent attention stems from our tax fetish, and Canadians have traditionally been excessively tax-driven in their pursuit of offshore opportunities. Unfortunately, taxes are only one part of the equation. As a result, many people have missed other advantages that offshore business and financial planning can offer. But more to the point, tax-free or for that matter tax-deferred offshore opportunities are increasingly becoming non-existent as government revenue authorities circle the wagons in their efforts to stem the flow of funds from Canada.

The most important thing to understand about offshore is that, ultimately, the only true means by which a Canadian can achieve tax-free status is to leave Canada. The trend toward becoming a non-resident of Canada and establishing permanent residence elsewhere, such as a tax-free or tax-efficient jurisdiction, while almost unheard of 15 years ago, is becoming an increasingly attractive alternative. Admittedly, becoming a non-resident means cutting most formal financial ties with Canada. But if it is well planned, non-residency doesn't entail enforced exile from a personal, social or even lifestyle point of view. What's more, many of the advantages of Canadian residency, such as the healthcare system, can be secured through private medical insurance plans at a net cost savings compared to the income tax bite that is actually funding this "free" benefit. In addition, offshore brings other benefits besides simple freedom from taxation, as we shall see.

Demographics is playing an unprecedented part in our daily lives and an even larger part in the world of global finance and investment. We are healthier and living longer than any previous generation. In fact, the possibility that many of us will spend more time in retirement than we did working has placed the need for personal financial planning in a whole new light. We are also becoming progressively richer as the largest transference of wealth in Canadian history—Professor Foot's $1 trillion inheritance of *Boom, Bust & Echo* fame—will soon be upon us. With innovations in technology and communications washing over us like a giant electronic wave, we are also far more mobile than previous generations, which makes our ability to live and work anywhere in the world not just a dream but an easily attained reality.

This book is part study of offshore jurisdictions, structures and investment tools; part financial planning and investment guide; and part political/social commentary and examination of things to come. I trust that you will be able to put it to your offshore advantage.

Gordon Laight
Nassau, The Bahamas

PROLOGUE

the case of the high school land revisited

THE BEGINNING OF A PERSONAL ODYSSEY

Single out the big and moderately big properties for attack and very soon, as if by magic, they will begin to avoid you and disappear, as all things in the world very reasonably do when they are singled out for attack. Even the half-starved crow will not wait to be continuously shot at.

—THE *TIMES* OF LONDON, MAY 17, 1894

In June 1997 on a business trip to Ottawa, I came down with a serious case of food poisoning from eating mussels. Food poisoning is something that ordinarily passes in 24 to 48 hours, but with mussels there is always the risk of hepatitis. Consequently, when we realized what was wrong, my wife and I immediately made our way to the local hospital. Since we were non-residents, I was obliged to hand over my American Express card when we checked in at the emergency room, which created some confusion since we were the only "paying" customers. The attending nurse told us that it was wise of us to come in because of the risks involved and that the visit would cost $275, excluding any procedures or medication. I was also told a doctor would see me shortly.

We waited and waited. After about an hour, we inquired as to how much longer it would be. The nurse looked at us, looked at the waiting room and looked at her watch, saying, "Well, if all goes well, about six or eight hours." I was already about seven pounds lighter than I had been some hours previously and now felt positively faint. Still, I summoned the strength to ask, "What if I had come by ambulance?" at which she pointed down the hall at a dozen or so people on gurneys and said, "They all came by ambulance."

My wife was furious and started making phone inquiries at other healthcare facilities, only to be told that we would have a similar wait there. By this time it was critical that we make a decision. In the end, my wife contacted Air Canada and moved our flight up to the next one available. Thanks to the miracle of modern aviation, we were home in Nassau and at our family doctor's office in less time than it would have taken for the emergency room doctor to see me if we had waited in Canada. I was discharged with suitable medication in minutes and the visit cost only $50.

I am contrasting this story of healthcare in the Bahamas with Canada—offshore and onshore—for two reasons. Obviously, my wife and I, while Canadian citizens, live in Nassau. But this may also serve to illustrate the fact that a country with no taxation, subsidies, drug company lobbyists and a medical profession free to work, as it should, with little or no government intervention, can actually succeed in its endeavours where others seemingly do not or cannot. An offshore advantage, if you like.

Like many other shibboleths, the fears that Canadians express over the potential of a privatized medical system are in my view largely unfounded. Nonetheless, we realized that in the time since we had left Canada, we had not experienced the healthcare cuts and hospital closings at first hand. They have clearly had a demoralizing impact. However, medicine is a business like any other, and should feel the effects of supply and demand. The same should apply to specialists, drugs and medical procedures. Consider this: Erythromycin, a common antibiotic, is approximately $65 in Canada yet costs only $16 in the Bahamas. If you have children with asthma, you would be familiar with Ventalin, which costs in excess of $20 in Canada, but just $6 in the Bahamas.

Why is this true? And why, for example, should our Canadian hospital visit have cost $275 when the Bahamian equivalent was just $50? In two words, less government. In this context, consider that about 40% of your provincial tax bill goes to fund your public healthcare system. Also consider what my private and universally accepted family medical coverage costs: about US$2,000 per year. Calculate 40% of your provincial tax bill, and see who's really ahead.

With less government, there is less redistribution of private wealth by a costly and inefficient governmental middleman or infrastructure. Healthcare in Canada may be a case in point, where ideology has got in the way of delivery, and where the worship of costly, crumbling hospital buildings—mostly constructed in the 1950s but on which "tradition" has conferred institutional status a little like Renaissance Italian churches or Oxford colleges—gets in the way of patient care. In any event, it is certainly a defining difference between onshore and offshore.

The Case for Critical Self-Examination

My wife and I have been living offshore for several years now and have no intention of returning to Canada in the near future. We are part of the large Canadian community in Nassau, which consists of professional expatriates as well as retired and independently wealthy Canadians. This situation is not unique to Nassau, and there are over 700 islands in the Bahamas with Canadians on almost all of them. Equally, there are Canadian expatriate communities throughout the Caribbean.

While I live offshore by choice, my Canadian roots go deep. That's why it disturbs me when a great country trips and fails to live up to its promise. This is especially true in the global world in which so much of the rest of humanity is happily and profitably living. Many years ago, the poet Earle Birney captured the essence of our provincialism: the case of the high school land, dead set in adolescence.

So let's take a closer look at ourselves and consider the lie of the land onshore before thinking about moving off. Canada is the second-largest land mass in the world next to Russia, yet we have a total population of only approximately 35 million people (32 million live in California). Over 60% of our population base is situated in the St. Lawrence corridor between Quebec City and Windsor, Ontario. That makes us a thinly populated country given the sheer mass of our geography. From the Atlantic to the Pacific, but with almost the same population as California, the resources needed to maintain and grow Canada are great, but unfortunately economies of scale do not work in our favour.

Is it any wonder that over the past few years the concept of a decentralized national government has become a reality? The resultant offloading of federal mandates and responsibilities to the provinces has occurred at a rapid pace and is nearly complete. What this has indirectly created is a series of economic zones which will have to work hard to defend their individual merits in order to make themselves attractive to business and industry, and increase employment and subsequently government revenue.

Due to its intrinsic ties of trade and commerce with the Pacific Rim, British Columbia has more in common with the American northwest and Asia than it does or ever will again with the rest of Canada. Alberta is starting to reap the benefits of Premier Klein's austerity measures in the form of fiscal surpluses, and when the price of oil begins its ascent again the province will truly have financial muscle. Atlantic Canada has seemingly turned its back on its small-C conservative past, and is embracing 1960s Swedish-style socialism. The worries and problems over the secession of Quebec that have plagued Canada for generations are just the tip of the iceberg as we approach the millennium. With a decentralized government and consequently provinces with greater economic and legislative independence, the idea of a series of sovereign "states" within Canada is not as far-fetched as you might imagine.

Canada's national identity has traditionally been forged by three primary areas of commonality: universal access to education, state-of-the-art healthcare and a participatory federal pension plan system (with Quebec opting out, as usual). This social safety net was the envy of the world. All three components of that net were originally financed and maintained through the centralized government's taxing power. But today, clearly the net needs mending.

What's happened here? Is government no longer supporting people? If not, what is the solution for the individual? Not to support government through tax evasion? Tax avoidance? Non-residency? Or is there an offshore advantage for many Canadians if only they realized it? These are some of the questions that we will attempt to explore.

THE ART OF TAXATION CONSISTS OF SO PLUCKING THE GOOSE TO OBTAIN THE LARGEST AMOUNT OF FEATHERS WITH THE LEAST POSSIBLE HISSING.

—J. B. Colbert, Comptroller General of Finance for Louis XIV

Healthcare, education and other aspects of the social safety net have consumed an enormous amount of the national wealth for generations. So has something else. A press release from the Fraser Institute published in April 1997 showed that Canadians have experienced a severe case of income tax inflation since 1961: while the CPI increased about 450% in this period, taxation skyrocketed almost 1,200%.[1]

Excessive taxation is not a new phenomenon nor is it endemic to Canada. Many democracies create highly complex, inefficient, unfair, confusing, confiscatory, lobby-driven tax systems that ignore sound economic principles and commercial reality. For example, in the United Kingdom in 1974, the top marginal rate of personal income tax was 83% on earned income and 98% on "unearned" or investment income. But the yield or actual amount collected by government was only 17.5% of total personal income because there were over 80 different deductions and allowances permitted by the tax code. What segment of the population paid the top marginal rate? Not the poor, since they were protected. Not the rich or well-advised because they could take advantage of the 80 deductions and allowances rates. Clearly, the middle class bore the brunt of this excessive tax bite.[2, 3]

MOST PEOPLE WHO FLEE TO TAX HAVENS DO SO BECAUSE THEY ARE FED UP WITH THE FISCAL OR TAX LAWS OF THEIR HOMELAND. THE MULTIMILLIONAIRE E. P. TAYLOR WAS SAID TO HAVE MOVED TO THE BAHAMAS TO AVOID CANADA'S HARSH WINTERS. EVERYONE KNOWS HE REALLY LEFT TO AVOID CANADA'S HARSH TAXES.

—Unattributed

Taxing Matters

Taxation as expressed in terms of marginal rates on earned income is bad enough. But if you want to understand your true level of taxation, consider this: taxation should be expressed as income less all government charges. In fact, income taxes actually represent less than half of your total annual tax bill. Look at your pay stub or tax return. Mandatory contributions to employment insurance (EI); mandatory and ever-increasing contributions to the Canada Pension Plan (CPP) (which currently sports a $150 billion unfunded liability); federal Goods and Services Tax (GST) and provincial sales tax; and what about fuel surtaxes, medical surtaxes, provincial surtaxes, federal surtaxes and municipal property taxes? Taxes other than income tax account for over 60% of the total annual tax bill of the average Canadian family.

With what's left you have to consider your standard of living. And finally you have to consider your retirement. If you try to save for your financial future outside a tax-deferred plan (i.e., RRSP), income is taxed at your top marginal rate, capital gains are taxed at 75% of the gain, while dividends are only slightly preferentially taxed. Even the sanctity of RRSPs themselves may be in question. You may recall that prior to the release of the 1995 federal budget, there were a few well-placed articles in the nation's press hinting that RRSPs may be taxed on either a contribution or growth—not just deregistration or conversion—basis. The uproar was sufficient to get the government to pull in its horns, but the idea is still being considered. The constriction of annual contribution limits is another form of increased taxation in and of itself. Less income can now be sheltered in an RRSP, which leaves more income to be freely taxed. The return of estate taxes is yet another area of immediate concern for Canadians—federally mandated estate taxes, mind you, not the easily circumvented, provincially regulated system that was in effect until 1972. In fact, the government already taxes unrealized capital gains at death unless assets are transferred directly or rolled over to a spouse.

The reduction from $500,000 to $100,000 and subsequent elimination of the capital gains exemption was another ill-conceived blow for the Canadian taxpayer. Many people shrugged off the elimination of the exemption at the time, but if you have been wise enough to take advantage of the bull market of the past eight years, you are doubtless sitting on some sizable taxable gains and may well wish you still had an offset for them.

What all this taxing activity has created is a precarious balancing act for many Canadians. The demand and subsequent overexpansion of credit of the past decade has resulted in personal debt levels never before seen. Personal bankruptcies are at an all-time high and continue to rise. People are balancing a series of maxed-out credit cards and lines of credit from month to month just to live; worse still, many people have taken out home equity loans or second mortgages to invest in the market. Why? The reason is disposable income, or, more to the point, the lack thereof. Taxation now accounts for more of the average Canadian's budget than food, shelter and clothing combined. People are using debt just to live. Why are many individuals increasing their personal debt loads at such a mind-numbing pace? Because interest rates are at generational lows and refinancing accumulated debt has never been easier.

But this type of leverage is dangerous. The next economic slowdown or recession will be the equivalent of a massive margin call, and many people who have leveraged their homes to invest in the market will lose their investment and the ownership of their house as well. It is an act of pure professional irresponsibility that some financial planners persist in recommending this strategy.

THE MEASURE OF SUCCESS IS NOT WHETHER YOU HAVE A TOUGH PROBLEM TO DEAL WITH, BUT WHETHER IT'S THE SAME PROBLEM YOU HAD LAST YEAR.

—John Foster Dulles

The wonder that surrounds the global economic boom of the 1990s has largely been the result of technology. The information, communications and automation advances of the past decade have created an economic environment of staggering potential. If an entrepreneur thirty years ago was experiencing increased regional competition, market saturation or recession, it would have been difficult to seek out new customers in Europe or Asia unless that individual was very well connected or had very deep pockets. Today, the entrepreneur has global fax, cellular and Internet capabilities, which can transcend borders at the roll of a mouse and stroke of a keyboard to create instant international commerce. The global investor is now in much the same position.

Such economic freedom grates on the nerves of many North American politicians, who would still like nothing more than to control and eventually levy taxes and government surcharges on the ability of individuals and corporations to conduct their affairs in the new paradigm. It is not coincidental that a tax on the Internet has already been proposed. Canadians as much as other people worldwide have been affected by this kind of tax-and-spend worldview expressed and enacted by their legislators.

While offshore is not exclusively about taxation, it is a component—a complex component—in the equation. But offshore is also about freedom, choice and opportunity. This book will explore where offshore is and what it can do, in providing you with many options to enable you to deal effectively with the new economic order.

CHAPTER 1

the emergence of THE GLOBAL CITIZEN

I am a citizen, not of Athens or Greece, but of the world.

—SOCRATES QUOTED IN PLUTARCH, *DE EXILIO*, V.

It is increasingly commonplace to meet and conduct business with people who were born in one country, educated in another, are now living in yet another and have business interests in all three—as well as in many other nations besides. These individuals are not necessarily unique; nor is this any longer just a small number of people in any given population group. Traditionally, the emigration and redistribution of people from an impoverished or oppressive country to a more desirable one has produced massive social and economic change, as witness the U.S. experience late in the last century. As Bosnia and other recent history shows, this process will continue as we move forward through time. But the new emigration is different in that it is not now largely a mass movement; rather, it reflects the needs of the autonomous individual.

Throughout history, we have been conditioned to believe that people are essentially limited in terms of mobility to their own given country and usually venture outside only for vacation and leisure purposes; hence the immobility of people and their assets has formed the way we see the world both socially and from a business perspective. For example, not so long ago, the entrepreneur or small business owner had little opportunity to compete on a national basis, let alone internationally. The typical business was largely confined to its city or region and would live or die on the basis of the economy of that locale alone. But demographics and the information age are changing our antiquated views of economics and geopolitics.[4]

Of most immediate interest for our purposes, people are no longer obliged to live in jurisdictions that impose high rates of taxation in order to earn income or generate national wealth. Governments in high-tax jurisdictions are, in effect, losing their best "customers" to jurisdictions that operate on a fairer or no-tax basis. The ability to redistribute wealth effectively in Canada and nations like Canada has been checked by the need to tax at excessive levels to service the accumulated government debt, which has been the only tangible result of the wealth redistribution process. But herein lies the paradox. The technological and information revolution gives anyone with a computer and a communications conduit the ability to conduct any information-based business or move vast sums of money in complex financial transactions anywhere in the world. The most conspicuous characteristic of the modern nation state, which is its taxing power, is thus being eroded by technology at a time when it needs its tax revenue most.

The New Global Capital

It has been said that, if the late 20th century's political contribution to history has been balkanization, the legacy for financial markets has decidedly been globalization.

Ask your parents or even grandparents how many Asian or European investment holdings they had access to in their prime investing years. Outside of the professional or institutional investor, few had access to stocks that today constitute leading global indices, such as Germany's DAX, the United Kingdom's FTSE 100, Japan's Nikkei 225, Hong Kong's Hang Seng, Mexico's Bolsa or Brazil's Bovespa. More importantly, many of the leading international stock exchanges scarcely existed as they do today. Generally, the world's financial centres were restricted to North America and western Europe where the tradition of commerce, finance and administrative systems were strongest. Those who ventured farther afield earlier in the 20th century, aside from a few investment pioneers such as Sir John Templeton, were largely private sector businessmen and multinational corporations. Now that has all changed.

The roots of the new global investment marketplace spring from the liberalization and growth of international trade flows beginning after the Second World War, and more directly as a result of the progress of the GATT negotiations and growing economic interdependence. One key result has been the commoditization of financial markets, a trend that has discernibly altered the way multinational corporations, financial institutions, central banks and governments interact. Commoditization has meant that control over the financial superhighway is now fragmented by myriad daily transactions, not just the market influence of central banks, large pension funds or George Soros–style speculators. Commoditization of financial markets has also meant that international fund flows—executed by electronic technology and derivative mathematics—now transcend individual world markets. A bull or bear market in any financial asset class can now be passed simultaneously through each time zone, resulting in synchronized market moves around the clock, around the globe. Witness the global equity market collapse of 1987, the emerging markets euphoria of the early 1990s or the Mexican peso crisis in late 1994. Even the international benchmark of liquidity, the U.S. dollar, has become commoditized by global currency traders.

Underlying these trends has been the phenomenal growth of derivatives, which quantitatively determine the relationships between an underlying market or security and its definable components, and unbundle those components in respect of risk and price. Innovation in technology has meant that time zones no longer exist in the capital markets, information flows and trade execution are instantaneous, and the daily velocity of international currency transactions now transcends the GDP or wealth of most nations. There is also some irony in the fact that a U.S. or international investor can benefit from the full protection of the Commodity Futures

Trading Commission (CFTC) or Securities and Exchange Commission (SEC) without encountering the hand of the regulator—or the tax collector—at all. It is equally unsurprising that the Cayman Islands are home to more Eurodollar deposits than any other country in the world.

Through the longest-running bull market in history and concurrent boom in the mutual fund and financial planning industries during the 1980s and 1990s, Canadian investors have embraced the "global" investment opportunity, which is really just another word for offshore. The principal reason isn't hard to find: Canada makes up less than 3% of the world's total equity market capitalization and only slightly more of the globe's fixed-income marketplace. This realization, plus the gradual increases in foreign content room in RRSPs from 1992 to the present (the rate has basically doubled), have given rise to new fund launches that cover Far East, Asia Pacific, Latin American and European equity and bond markets. But bringing the world to your investment portfolio has not been just clever marketing on the part of Canada's financial institutions and wealth managers. In fact, the recent crop of international funds have been among the best investment opportunities to hit Canadian shores since those double-digit GICs of days gone by.

But Canadians have experienced some structural problems in benefiting from the new global financial marketplace. For starters, investors are limited to a maximum of only 20% allowable foreign content in their RRSPs. Which is ironic, because, after all, everyone has access to global fund or investment opportunities through newspapers and periodicals or via one of the many global investment Web sites. The sad truth is that, if Canada makes up less than 3% of the world's total equity market capitalization, theoretically 97% of the world's investment opportunities have yet to be examined or experienced by Canadian investors.

In addition, it is also ironic that many Canadians are only now coming to terms with the idea that equities themselves are not such a bad thing, and that a diversified portfolio means more than buying GICs to complement their Canada Savings Bonds. This has been partially a result of conditioning, but more importantly reflects a misunderstanding of the real meaning of investment risk, which not only means market volatility but also embraces considerations such as comparative performance and reinvestment risk.

As a result of the declining interest rate environment in North America essentially since 1982, Canadian investors have been forced to examine the investment opportunities that exist beyond Treasury bills and GICs. It's not greed, it's been necessity. Three or four percent per annum doesn't go very far these days. Unfortunately, the majority of investors' alternative investment options are concentrated both on and in Canada. As we have seen, not only is the Canadian equity market small in global terms, but also it still has a heavy concentration in the natural resource sector and only modest representation from the mature industrial, high-tech and service sectors. For example, the TSE 300 Composite Index has about twice the exposure to basic industries, the proverbial rocks and trees, as does the U.S. big-cap S&P 500 Index. Hence Canada is still an inflation-oriented market.

When increased global demand for natural resources and raw materials starts to heat up, it is usually at the end of a period of economic expansion. During this time, inventories are shrinking, or have been depleted, demand for raw materials increases and the price of those raw materials begins to rise, causing the prices of finished goods to rise as well (a.k.a. inflation). The central banks and finance ministries know inflation is bad, so they raise interest rates which indirectly (through the increased cost of financing) raises the price of finished goods even further. Throughout this process, the world starts to rediscover a commodity-based economy such as Canada, and you witness a tremendous amount of foreign buying of Canadian equities, which in turn places increased cyclical pressure on the Canadian equity marketplace. The problem is that when many Canadians see foreigners buying up all the Canadian equities they can get their hands on, they think that it must be the time to buy. Wrong! The principal sellers are usually domestic institutional and mutual fund managers who are adept at rotating out of the resource and cyclical sectors when they sense the party is over. In turn, individual Canadians find that their RRSPs are left holding the bag after the foreign investors have taken their profits and gone elsewhere or rediscovered the bond market. Foreign investors have long understood the value of global investing and how to do so successfully. After all, they still have 97% of the world's investment opportunities to pursue.

Closer to Home—Alarm Bells Should Be Ringing

Against this global backdrop, there is trouble brewing at home. The United States is just beginning to acknowledge the fact that, on the basis of actuarial calculations, the Social Security system will have a serious shortfall by the year 2029. That doesn't mean it will be broke. It does mean that the taxes that pay for the benefit cheques issued to retirees will be sufficient to cover only about 75% of annual expenditures. President Clinton has suggested reserving 100% of the expected 1999 budget surplus until a solution to the Social Security problem is at hand. But the problem with setting aside budget surpluses is twofold. Number one, you are not paying down debt; and number two, you are not investing in the country's future. The Republicans are building their case for a private retirement system that would at first supplement and eventually replace the existing public system.

The Canadian government has yet to fully acknowledge that it has a similar problem. The Canada Pension Plan is also in dire straits, as it currently has a $150 billion unfunded liability. Mandatory contributions in Canada have increased substantially over the past ten years, but still no relief has been found. Again, demographics or the aging of North America has and will have a great deal to do with any possible solutions.

After the Second World War, men in their twenties came home, found work, got married and began fathering children. Hence the baby boom of 1946–1966, when approximately 100 million people were born in North America. These same baby boomers are now the largest segment of the population and they are aging. Actuaries are now becoming concerned about the future shortage of workers who will pay taxes to provide the benefits for retiring baby boomers. In 1950 the ratio of workers to retirees was 16 to 1. By the year 2025 that ratio is expected to be 2 to 1. The second concern on the mind of actuaries is the longevity of the baby boomers. In the 1930s and 1940s, the average life expectancy for males was 61.7 years; today it is 77 years. People are healthier, living longer and retiring younger than ever before. That means the boomers will be around a lot longer to collect a lot more Social Security and CPP, creating the possibility of an accelerated drain on the respective systems, which were created in the 1960s.

This is where the individual investor should have a sense of foreboding. Many people mistakenly think that Social Security and CPP are a return, plus interest, of the payroll contributions and taxes they have paid over their working life. We've all said it or heard it said: "I plan to get out exactly what I put in." This is a total misconception. In point of fact, it is from the wages of today's workers that today's beneficiaries are paid. And it will be the workers of the year 2025 who will pay the benefits of their retired colleagues in 2025: the same individuals who will make up that ratio of 2 workers to every 1 retired person (imagine what their real tax liability will be). Social Security and CPP are not actuarially funded investment programs; in essence, they are social insurance programs.

The questions being raised and range of possible solutions include giving people the ability to opt out of these plans and provide for their own retirement, or a possible two-tier system under which an individual's contributions are split between the public system and a private account. Another suggestion is to defer the age at which people can begin to collect benefits. But the political will to effect change will be difficult to raise, as a rational response to deficit funding always seems to smack of elitism to the Canadian electorate.

The American Association of Retired Persons (AARP) and its Canadian counterpart (CARP) are large lobby groups and its members carry many more votes than their grandchildren, so there will probably be no solution at all. More important is the mistaken assumption, made by governments and financial institutions alike, that senior citizens represent a single demographic entity. My 80-year-old grandmother, for example, has nothing in common financially with my 65-year-old aunt any more than a Gen-Xer has with his or her parents. Some dangerous assumptions are going to be made by governments on behalf of North America's retirees and senior citizens as a result.

Of course it has been suggested that governments raise mandatory plan contribution levels or taxes or both. The problems that exist for these government plans are not going to be solved in the short term. Frequently, even sophisticated investors have not given this adequate consideration. Prudent individuals should be mapping out alternative investment and saving strategies to protect against the possible failure of these plans or at least augment their retirement income in future.

There is one very small light at the end of this very long tunnel for North American governments. It is becoming increasingly obvious that there may eventually be more jobs than people to fill them in the coming decade. The number of workers aged 25–44 is falling and the median age of the North American workforce will be over 40 by 2005; it was 34.7 in 1979. Every eight seconds, somebody in North America turns 50 and by 2025, all of North America may start to resemble a retirement home.[5] Or will it? The number of "seniors" either returning to the workforce or not leaving it is an interesting phenomenon. The media-driven idea that the boomers would retire early to tour the globe or pursue domestic endeavours full-time is clearly a load of rubbish, as were similar articles about boomers bouncing from career to career. The majority of these articles assumed that all boomers are financially advantaged. They are not. The fear of outliving their retirement savings is a motivating factor that is beginning to rear its ugly head to the conspicuous consumer boomers of the 1980s, as is the boredom of retirement itself. Many polls indicate that most baby boomers expect to be working past 65. While this may be a reprieve to the government, many companies have not thought about the prospect of having a much older workforce in the coming decades and the associated costs of caring for them.[6]

In virtue of these considerations, many pundits have pointed to immigration as a solution to the shrinking workforce, but for Canada specifically this may be a real problem. The June 21, 1998 *Vancouver Sun* had an article entitled "Canada sees sharp drop in Asian investor immigrants." It focused on the decrease in immigrant investors from Hong Kong and

Taiwan to Canada in 1997 (94% and 78% respectively). These numbers were apparently leaked from federal government sources. The main reason for the drop was the newly introduced foreign asset reporting rules, which Asian immigrant investors see as "discriminatory, invasive, inconvenient, costly to comply with and oppressive." What was more disturbing is that, according to these leaked details, the number of investor immigrants from all countries fell 38% between 1996 and 1997, including a whopping 72% decline in the first quarter of 1998 compared to the first quarter of 1997. So much for importing the skilled workforce of tomorrow.

Money Has Wings

The power of our information technology is changing economic and financial frontiers. The ability to move vast sums from one country, currency and asset class to another has empowered investors large and small to view the world in much different terms from that of any generation previously. This is also going to have a profound effect on the way governments of the Western world function in future. Global foreign exchange traders and investment managers now have the ability to discipline, sometimes severely, governments which are mismanaging their country's affairs or, worse, have fallen into misguided or even corrupt ways.

In 1997, Indonesia's fate was sealed by thousands of traders who saw the financial potential of investing in the country but also saw the nepotistic and corrupt government of President Suharto as the barrier to its success. In an example closer to home, Jean Charest's decision to run for the provincial Liberal leadership in Quebec was made with help from these same traders and managers, who warned publicly that the Canadian dollar would suffer if he decided to remain in federal politics. Increasingly, Canada's political and economic decisions will be based on just such opinion and pressure. For the same reason, Lucien Bouchard, the premier of Quebec, makes his now semiannual pilgrimages to New York to meet with Wall Street to negotiate and schmooze with the people who hold Quebec provincial bonds and permit ongoing investment in that province.

Canada, like every other sovereign state, needs foreign investment to build reserves and support the strength of its currency. Foreign investment will only flow if a country can demonstrate sound political and economic policies designed to maintain its strength and competitiveness. In essence, global foreign exchange traders and investment managers will only invest in countries where a rate of return commensurate with their risk expectations can be achieved. Today, they wield the financial power to effect policy and political decisions. This is a discipline that far exceeds that of the gold standard of thirty years ago. Governments are only beginning to come to the realization that they can no longer protect themselves against the fickle judgments of the financial world.

If you start thinking of Canada as you would a potential investment, you should start thinking about taxes as the cost of that investment. Do you make investments where the risks outweigh the potential returns? As an investor in Canada (i.e., a taxpayer), are you happy with the return on your investment? Do you feel the "company" is putting your money to good use? Can you expect to retire on your investment? As a prudent investor, you would want to see an annual report to examine the balance sheet and income statements for cash flow figures, net income, projected earnings, outstanding debt and the current P/E ratio. Should you become a shareholder activist and start asking the management team of the "company" some hard questions? Or should you limit your exposure to this investment and consider a strategy that could effectively diversify those assets you wish to protect? Start thinking in these terms and you will understand what foreign investors look for in a country when making global investment bets.

The Euro Is Coming! The Euro Is Coming!

There has been and will be more brouhaha about the imminent arrival of the Eurodollar. In short, the Euro is going to be the single, unified currency for the first 11 nation states of Western Europe, which is the end result of the European Union under the Maastricht Treaty. There are parties both for and against the unified currency. The coordination needed to implement the Euro is mind-boggling. Eleven separate tax, wage and interest rate systems must be merged, not to mention the social system changes that will have to take place. All this must be coordinated precisely to ensure the viability of the new unified currency.

The detractors of the Euro have made a few points worth considering. Europe is not a homogeneous society, and asking 11 nations with separate national agendas to come together under one currency could prove perilous. Take the strikes that have plagued France over the years: if they continue, they are going to have to be dealt with under the new, unified system. The continued high cost of absorbing the former East Germany will also have to be shared under a collective system. The leadership of the unified Europe is and will continue to be a contentious issue, and the possibility of a member state holding the union "hostage" by refusing to honour its obligations is a subject some want to avoid considering entirely. Even the politicking behind the selection of the president of the new European central bank made the Machiavellian Francis Urquhart in the BBC series about the manipulative prime minister look positively Sunday-schoolish.

Now for the bad news. If the Euro flies through its implementation phase and thereafter, the political and economic pressure on North America could be enormous. Under a strong unified currency, Europeans will not need to hold as many U.S. dollar reserves. There would also be a much larger shift into Euros by other sovereign nations. In fact, the role of the Euro as a potential reserve currency for this country has already been mooted by the Governor of the Bank of Canada. Such currency displacement would necessitate a shift in global economic power as the role of the greenback as the world's primary currency is challenged. The resulting pressure on and possible depreciation of the American dollar would put the United States under scrutiny by international traders and investment managers with negative implications for long-term U.S. interest rates and economic growth prospects.

These factors would also impact Canada negatively. The Canadian dollar would probably suffer the same fate as the U.S. currency, if not on a greater scale, considering the relative strength of the overall Canadian economy compared to its U.S. counterpart, let alone a unified European economy. Canada's global purchasing power parity would be further eroded by a weakened dollar, effectively imprisoning the population of Canada within its borders since venturing beyond them would be prohibitively expensive. Virtually no one would be driving imported cars or drinking French wine, either. The greater problem is the potential impact on the Canadian bond market, and hence long-term interest rates. Canada's bond market has traditionally been one of the world's safe havens, since Canada's debt instruments have always been rated highly and favoured by international investors because of their liquidity and the quality of the marketplace. Canada will soon have to compete for its share of the global bond market against a unified EuroLand.

Global economic events such as the birth of the Euro will be a catalyst for similar changes around the world. Imagine an Asian politicoeconomic alliance or a Latin American union. Regional governments will have to cooperate in order to maintain each individual country's viability. Japan is on the brink of total economic collapse with the latest calculations of its private and public debt amounting to nearly 250% of GDP; no wonder it is no longer viewed as the guiding force to lead the Asian markets in any alliance. Ironically, it may be the up-and-coming Asian countries which have learned some valuable lessons from Japan's bubble economy that will give Japan a leg up. Latin American countries, which are coincidentally canvassing to become part of the NAFTA agreement, are already seeking to create economic alliances among themselves. The old East/West political blocs are gone, but have been replaced by Asian, Latin, European and North American economic successors.

Investing for Success— The Offshore Alternative

For most of this decade, the unbridled success of the North American mutual fund industry has been wondrous to behold. If I had told you five years ago that some of the most successful mutual funds in the world would close their doors to new investors because they were too big, too unmanageable and consequently underperforming, I doubt you would have believed me. But suffice it to say that we have already seen mighty Fidelity close its Magellan, Growth & Income, Contra and other funds for exactly those reasons. Many other fund companies will follow suit. Once again, the reason is demographics. The world's baby boomers are entering their prime saving years, and with interest rates at generational lows, Treasury bills and fixed-rate investments are not an option. In fact, in the United States, the amount of money invested in mutual funds now exceeds what is on deposit at the banks. But this is going to slow down. Believe me now or read about it later.

The fact is, the majority of mutual fund managers have been lagging the leading equity index performance benchmarks such as the S&P 500 for a number of years now. Combine structural underperformance with the annual distribution of capital gains to investors, which creates an immediate tax liability, and their performance is further eroded. If you tack on the stiff annual management fees, it's no wonder that many high-net-worth investors have been looking for alternatives to funds. As the boomers get older and closer to retirement, maximum performance and minimal fees will be their battle cry.

Some solutions to the mutual fund performance problem have been created over the past few years. For example, exchange-traded, index-linked instruments like S&P 500 depository receipts or SPDRs—the logic being, why buy a fund whose benchmark is the S&P 500 when you can buy synthetic shares in the benchmark itself? Other index-linked products include Diamonds for the 30-stock Dow Jones Industrial Average and LEAPS (Long-term Equity Anticipation Shares) for individual companies and indexes, and more are currently being developed. Hedge funds are also growing in popularity as individual investors are looking for alternatives to traditional fund management techniques. Hedge fund managers seek to achieve a risk-adjusted rate of return by benefiting from both bullish and bearish price movements while utilizing various investment strategies. These funds can also be used to complement a portfolio of traditional equity and fixed-income investments.

Does this mean that investors should avoid mutual funds altogether? Absolutely not. The mutual fund universe is enormous, inhabited as it is by the great, the once-great and the not-so-great. You are simply going to have to be more judicious in your analysis and with your investment decisions; but with more funds than individual stocks now in North America, that's not so easy. Another solution is opening a privately managed account at a bank, brokerage or private money management firm, where you will receive personalized attention and have the ability to better manage your tax liability with an investment plan that is tailored to your needs. The investment minimums and costs associated with private money management have come down considerably in recent years, and if this trend continues as it should, you can expect costs to come down even further.

In the offshore world, private money management has been the norm for many years. Unfortunately, the private banks and trust companies that have dominated the offshore industry tended to feature relatively high costs and comparatively poor performance. But like their onshore counterparts, offshore banks are now being forced to become far more competitive thanks to an increasingly fee-sensitive clientele and increased competition from a rapidly growing contingent of international private money management and brokerage firms. This proliferation of choice is serving to shake up the staid private banking and trust environment, and with good cause. For too many years, offshore investors had to endure mediocre rates of return further eroded by a host of management, custodial and other fees.

In this and other ways, the offshore investment industry is changing rapidly. Offshore jurisdictions, their financial institutions and money managers are no longer the domain of criminals, dictators, drug dealers and their ill-gotten gains. The legislative initiatives of many jurisdictions in the past decade have served to raise the profile of offshore as a legitimate means of global diversification for businesses and individual investors. The performance track records of many offshore managers have also been a magnet for global capital. Combined with the advantages of holding financial assets through offshore structures, the development of a first-class investment management industry offshore may be the most important development in its long and checkered history.

CHAPTER 2

what is OFFSHORE?

In 1971, we were forced to make a decision courtesy of the British Government—live in England and (because of taxes) not be able to afford another set of guitar strings—or move and keep the band together. Hence "Exile on Main Street."

—RICHARD HARRINGTON, "STONE FREE," INTERVIEW WITH MICK JAGGER, *WASHINGTON POST*, NOVEMBER 11, 1988

Offshore must be one of the most maligned words in the financial world today, thanks in no small part to the media's fascination with it. From the stereotypical, heavyset, sweaty Mafiosi in John Grisham's *The Firm* to the politicians who endorse currency controls as a method of retaining financial assets within a given jurisdiction, offshore is as misunderstood as it is maligned.

But what precisely is offshore? The word *offshore* can mean many things, depending on whom you ask. Talk to a European and you will be told offshore is any place to conduct business that provides efficient access to foreign markets and is free from bureaucratic red tape. Tax advantages are usually secondary to the business benefits. Talk to someone from any politically oppressed nation, and you will be told that offshore provides a modicum of economic freedom that is otherwise not possible in their home jurisdiction. Talk to a Canadian and, rightly or wrongly, the conversation will focus entirely on taxes.

The truth is an amalgam of all these points of view. Offshore is anywhere that features a supportive regulatory and administrative environment, sophisticated financial and professional infrastructure, progressive legislation, advanced communications—and tax-efficiency. That's why the real challenge is not to think of offshore (a.k.a. international business and/or global investing) as a specific place, but instead as a state of mind. In other words, offshore is anywhere you are *not*.

It's hard for us to keep this in perspective, but for people living outside North America, Canada and the United States are considered offshore jurisdictions. Consider this: Toronto is one of the largest offshore mutual fund administration centres in the world. Thanks to the cheap dollar, Canada's banks and trust companies have carved out a profitable niche as administrator, custodian and banker for international fund and investment firms whose products are not available to individual investors in Canada.

Looking back in history, business people have been actively creating offshore opportunities for centuries. Shortly after the American Revolution, British and other European entrepreneurs recognized the advantages of doing business in a tax-free jurisdiction. After all, why was the American Revolutionary War fought? As a result, they established trading and shipping companies to exploit commerce with the newly liberated New World colonies. From a European investment perspective, Canada and the United States were effectively considered offshore throughout the 19th century not only because of the opportunities they provided to indulge in unfettered capitalism, but also because they were no-tax jurisdictions. In fact, it is arguable that the flow of immigrants to North America throughout the 18th and 19th centuries had more to do with escaping from oppressive political and taxing economic systems than any other reason. Hence the term of the time, *land of opportunity*.

But the real key to understanding offshore lies in the more recent past. Beginning in the 1950s, a strange new currency called the Eurodollar was born. Eurodollars are simply U.S. dollars on deposit with banks outside the United States, i.e., offshore. Their Cold War provenance, which dates from the time of the Korean War, might have been fodder for a novel by Ian Fleming. Because their own currencies were soft and the U.S. dollar had become the dominant vehicle after the Second World War for international trade, both the Russians and the Chinese maintained U.S. dollar deposits with various European banks. In that way, the two communist regimes had access to the dollars they needed for global trade and assurance that their funds were beyond the reach of the U.S. government. As various regimes, including the Iranians, Libyans, Cubans, et al., have discovered, a freeze on the U.S. assets of foreign depositors is a very effective weapon in the hands of Uncle Sam. In addition, the communist bloc was earning U.S. dollars in its own right from the sale of international commodities (e.g., oil and gold) which of course are priced in U.S. dollars. As a result, the communist offshore piggybank soon began to bulge at the seams.

In the late 1950s, recurring pressure on the British pound necessitated a change in the way the United Kingdom would conduct trade with the non-sterling bloc. By husbanding pounds and borrowing U.S. dollars from the Soviets and Chinese, large amounts of which were on deposit in the City of London, the British inadvertently helped create one of the largest capital markets in the world—not their own, but an offshore market for U.S. dollars domiciled abroad. The Euromarket had other advantages beyond being outside the reach of the U.S. authorities. The principal benefit was the cost of money. Removed from compliance with the rules and regulations of the U.S. central banking system, there was no requirement to reserve, which significantly reduced the cost of funds in the Euromarket.

Then something else happened to increase its attractiveness. In 1963, the U.S. government introduced a tax on foreign borrowers. Termed the *interest equalization tax*, it was effectively an alternative to raising U.S. interest rates at a time when economic fragility made such a move politically inexpedient. The impact on foreign borrowers was to increase the cost of U.S. dollars borrowed in the United States—which gave the Euromarket a further shot in the arm. In time, not only did foreigners borrow in the Euromarket, but major U.S. corporations and financial institutions also became dominant players. Today, the Euromarket is pre-eminent among the world's capital markets in terms of both new issuance of securities and turnover (secondary trading).

The development of the Euromarket is a classic offshore paradigm: Russian gold as product to be sold or portfolio to be managed; U.S. dollars as medium of exchange; European banks as domicile or offshore jurisdiction; etc., etc. What should be clear, however, from this example is that offshore is not a place—it's a universe. The glue that makes offshore jurisdictions work is the concept of the offshore financial centre, which provides the banking, trust, brokerage and asset management services investors expect at home, with the added benefits of a regulatory, tax and investment environment that favours the accumulation and growth of wealth. But what London, Paris or Geneva provided for world capital in years gone by is now being served by much smaller and more diverse jurisdictions. For example, there are currently over 400 international and private banks, trust companies and investment firms located in the Bahamas, including many Canadian, U.S. and European brand names. Similarly, the Cayman is the most overbanked jurisdiction in the world, with an amazingly high ratio of financial institutions per capita of population. Tiny Western Samoa in the South Pacific also boasts more banks than many good-sized Canadian cities.

Like the concept of the Eurodollar in the 1950s, all offshore means, speaking strictly in an investment context, is holding ("domiciling") financial or real property assets outside an investor's country of residence. Offshore can be as simple as owning a house or vacation property somewhere in the world other than Canada and having the associated bank or financial accounts to deal effectively with the mortgage, maintenance and sundry needs of the property. For another individual, offshore can take the form of creating an asset protection structure against divorce or business partnership problems, or as a form of professional liability insurance. For the investor, offshore entails holding an existing portfolio—or building a new one—through an investment advisor or structure that is managed and physically held ("custodied") offshore. Offshore can also be effectively used in conducting global business by establishing an offshore branch or agency office to handle the international component of a particular business. In its ultimate application, many individuals are considering moving everything—business, family, money, everything—to an offshore jurisdiction from which to conduct their businesses and enjoy their lives.

This is not as far-fetched as it sounds. The ranks of Canadian families and business people moving to Nassau, for example, have swelled in recent years. A good friend of mine who lives a few doors away from my wife and me in Nassau is typical. He works for a Canadian telecommunications firm and is part of a team that services his company's global clientele. He is very happy to be living and working from Nassau. As he told me (this is verbatim), "The ability to be responsible and self-reliant in the areas of daily living, choice of healthcare, level of health insurance protection and the freedom to plan for my retirement any way I please is very liberating. If I lose my job tomorrow, there is no employment insurance to fall back on, so we stick to a strict budget and maintain a considerable level of savings, which is something I didn't do back in Canada. Interestingly enough, my parents are happy to see me living and working this way, as my father said this is how they lived in Canada before the rise of the social spending and the welfare state we have today."

But moving offshore and consequently becoming a non-resident of Canada is more than a just a business or tax consideration. Lifestyle should play an important, if not the most important, role, since lifestyle will be impacted most. It seems, however, that many people are prepared to take the plunge. Just to get a sense of the traffic flow, I recently asked for some statistics from a number of Canadian-based international moving companies. I had suspected but was still surprised to learn that, according to the three largest companies that specialize in this area, for every three people moving out of Canada, only one is moving in. Granted, these statistics were not gathered or quantified by scientific means; I simply asked the people who specialize in international moves for their ratios. You can take that as you will or you may want to read that *Vancouver Sun* article I referenced earlier.

What Offshore Is Not

Contrary to press reports, offshore is not a recent phenomenon; in fact, it has been utilized for centuries as a means of protecting financial assets, expanding business opportunities and generating wealth. But much of the hysteria that surrounds offshore, particularly in Canada, has been generated by a fundamental lack of understanding of its nature and applications.

To illustrate what offshore is not, or should not be, I started attending some of the many offshore investment seminars regularly conducted across Canada when I began working in the offshore advisory arena. One seminar in Montreal was made up of a panel of tax attorneys, chartered accountants and an investment manager from Bermuda. After paying $50 at the front door to attend, I sat down with a lawyer friend who had joined me and, pen and paper in hand, prepared to take copious notes. After an hour of listening, among other things, to a futures trader explain all the ways he could create sky-high returns for potential investors tax-free, it was time for questions. One astute investor asked how the investment programs that had been highlighted dealt with the Foreign Accrual Property Income (FAPI) rules as laid down by Revenue Canada. After several uncomfortable moments of silence, the tax attorney on the panel, from a well-respected and well-known Montreal law firm, rose and said, "I don't know that much about FAPI, but I will give it my best shot." Needless to say, the response fell far short of the investor's expectations.

There is nothing like misinformation to misinform, but nothing misinforms as much as ignorance. That's why the quest for offshore must begin with a clear exposition of each individual investor's goals and be executed in consultation with recognized, expert legal and financial planners in a manner consistent with those goals. Sounds all too familiar? Sounds, in fact, like the first principle of all financial planning? Unfortunately, it is simply the case that there are no cookie-cutter or "one size fits all" solutions to investing offshore, which is why offshore seminars fail to satiate the attendee's appetite for guidance. Don't get me wrong: offshore seminars are a great place to begin, but they can never be a source of immediate solutions. Effective solutions can only be provided to those individuals or businesses prepared to subject themselves to the scrutiny and advice of qualified advisors. Be prepared to answer a lot of questions and provide far more information than you ever provided to your domestic advisors. The perfect offshore plan has to be perfect for you.

Part of the planning process necessarily requires knowing your way around the various offshore jurisdictions, because it must be conceded that many domiciles and their financial institutions merited the bad press they received in the past. This is clearly not the offshore where you want to be. In many of the smaller, less important jurisdictions, anyone used to be allowed to conduct whatever business they pleased with no questions asked. But the worldwide legislative initiatives of the past decade to stem the flow of illicit funds, particularly from drug trafficking, have effectively enabled individuals to identify and avoid jurisdictions that operated on the fast-and-loose end of the spectrum in favour of those that meet the proper and conservative criteria of international banking and finance. Many of these legislative initiatives have been implemented with an eye to placing the onus on the financial institutions themselves to maintain the integrity of their clientele and therefore the jurisdiction itself. In fact, it can be safely said that today there are no unregulated jurisdictions in which or from which the international ne'er-do-well can operate without fear of being discovered.

Under the money laundering and fraudulent dispositions or conveyance legislation enacted in many offshore jurisdictions, if a banker allows a criminal or drug dealer to use his or her bank to conduct affairs (or more importantly, bank any proceeds from any criminal activity), the banker could be held personally responsible and convicted as an accessory to the relevant criminal activity. This has actually happened in a few jurisdictions to date and served as fair warning to all other financial institutions in the offshore community. Such legislation has gone a long way to improving the standards and practices of financial institutions worldwide and also clearly serves the needs of the legitimate investor and business person.

As many old timers will tell you, when a client used to walk into an offshore bank with a satchel full of money in the "good old days," a banker's time would be spent counting and arranging bank notes into neat, organized piles to be put on deposit in the vault. But today that client has gone elsewhere or to jail, and cash is no longer king. Very few institutions will accept cash transactions anymore (though there is no reporting requirement as in the United States, generally deposits of no more than US$10,000 and in many cases US$5,000 are the norm). Any offshore bank that will still do so would be ranked at the low end of the list of reputable practitioners.

Why Go Offshore?

Several years ago, a friend of mine who was brokering the biggest deal of his life, a large transaction between two prominent international companies, called me from his office in Vancouver to say that the deal was imminent and that his $1,000,000 fee was in the bag. When he could make the time, he told me that he wanted to sit down to discuss his offshore strategy. I had implored him to start planning for this event a year previously, but he kept putting it off because the deal was his primary concern and his life for the foreseeable future.

When the deal finally went through and his fee was paid, he called to say that now he was ready to sit down and plan. I asked where and when the fee would be paid. The answer: the money was already in the bank in Vancouver. I told him that I could have helped him $500,000 ago, but that $1 million was personal income less minor business disbursements and would be fully taxed. He had effectively put the cart before the horse.

Since this financial planning mishap, he has established a fully functional international subsidiary of his company in an offshore jurisdiction with a complete management and administrative staff. This company is responsible for the management and completion of all international transactions, while his Canadian company continues to conduct business in Canada and the United States. Funds paid to him in Canada from the international company as fees are declared as Canadian income and taxed accordingly. However, the international company now retains and invests the majority of its international income offshore, compounding free from taxes and benefiting from an unfettered range of global investment opportunities.

Like the broker from Vancouver, there are many legitimate reasons why individuals should consider looking offshore. Some of the most common, which will be considered in further detail throughout this book, are:

- Tax planning to reduce, defer or otherwise mitigate the effect of taxation
- Asset protection and immunity from creditors, including wives, mistresses, husbands, lovers, etc.
- More flexible environment to conduct business that minimizes bureaucracy but does not undermine legitimacy
- Access to professional expertise in accounting, finance and the law with a truly global view
- Double tax treaties—probably the most overlooked area by Canadians and retiring(ed) Canadians
- Higher investment performance on the basis of access to diversified, global investment opportunities
- Investor privacy and confidentiality
- Financial and estate planning flexibility

As previously noted, the primary things that investors are looking for in any offshore jurisdiction include a supportive regulatory environment, domestic tax-free or low-tax status and sophisticated financial infrastructure, including the possibilities afforded by bilateral tax agreements. Besides serving private clients and individual investors, most jurisdictions also specialize in the corporate and institutional market in areas such as offshore company formation, trusts, captive insurance, discretionary fund management, mutual fund administration and other related areas.

Despite all the legislative and regulatory progress of the past decade, there remain practices that, though unethical, still commonly occur, largely as a result of the difficulty of enforcing the "know your client" rule in an offshore context. The irony is that many people spend a great deal of time, effort and money to erect elaborate and dubious offshore structures only to find that they have in fact created a liability for themselves, their heirs and their beneficiaries.

In considering offshore, logic, not emotion, must be the guiding factor throughout your decision-making process. How many times I have heard this: "I'm tired of paying so much in taxes. I'll never be able to save for my retirement and the kids' education. I'm going to sell the house, deregister my RRSP, liquidate my investment account and transfer the whole lot offshore into a bank account and offshore funds. Then I'll rent a condo, lease a car and continue to transfer my remaining business assets offshore and no one will be the wiser." Yeah, sure! Your wife will leave you for selling the house, your kids will hate you for moving away from their friends, and Revenue Canada auditors will set up a tent on your front lawn while they conduct a lifestyle audit after you have effected your little plan.

Offshore jurisdictions can allow you to mitigate your tax burden, protect assets, plan for retirement and your estate needs or conduct business more efficiently, thereby creating an economic advantage. But it is crucial to understand that offshore should only be considered after all your domestic options have been exhausted. "Tax-free" offshore opportunities may or may not be possible depending on your individual circumstances, but a reduction of your personal and/or business's current tax burden is at least probable. However, as long as an individual remains a resident of Canada, he or she is subject to the laws of Canada and therefore must report all worldwide income (this has always been the case). Simply setting up a corporate structure in an offshore jurisdiction and transferring assets to it does not necessarily mitigate your tax liability. The structure itself is defined as a controlled foreign affiliate and the company and the individual contributing to it could be treated as one person for tax purposes. Before embarking offshore, you need to first analyze the fundamentals of your situation and identify all possible alternatives. I also cannot stress this enough: do your research and perform more than adequate due diligence on any potential offshore advisor you are considering. And do your homework before you even consider engaging the services of an offshore advisor.

Where Is Offshore?

It is estimated that as much as half the world's money either now resides in or passes through offshore jurisdictions (not a difficult task considering that there are in excess of forty countries counted as offshore or tax havens). Offshore jurisdictions have become an integral part of the world financial scene and this trend will continue over the foreseeable future. Their existence is no accident or aberration.

Offshore jurisdictions could not exist without the blessing of the world's major onshore powers and will only continue to survive at their whim. Many of the Caribbean offshore jurisdictions were created by the United Kingdom in the 1930s and 1940s in order to foster economic growth in what were then considered Third World countries. It was thought that by encouraging business in these areas, the home government would not have to inject as much "foreign aid" and could therefore save funds for other areas of spending, presumably of a more pressing nature and closer to home. The side benefit for companies that utilized these jurisdictions would be to receive substantial tax breaks on their overseas business ventures if they followed the rules. While this strategy did serve its purposes, no one foresaw the uses that these jurisdictions would be put to in future.

Anyone who thinks that offshore jurisdictions can legislate themselves into havens of absolute secrecy where the disclosure of information is criminal, and therefore confidentiality absolute, is mistaken. Just ask the Bank of Nova Scotia. About ten years ago, the U.S. courts asked the Bank to provide information on one of its Cayman-domiciled accounts. The Bank refused, citing Cayman secrecy laws. The U.S. court simply ignored the Cayman law and advised the Bank that it would impose a large daily fine on their New York office unless it complied. The bank capitulated after several days. Essentially the same situation occurred, this time in the Bahamas, with a client of the Ansbacher Bank that the U.S. government was examining. The U.S. government threatened to close Ansbacher's U.S. operations unless information concerning the client was forwarded by the Bahamian operation to the U.S. authorities. Ansbacher capitulated.

To cite another example, in the 1960s, France's President de Gaulle assumed that neighbouring Monaco was being used for widespread evasion of French taxation. He insisted that France should have extraterritorial taxation powers in Monaco in relation to French citizens. Monaco refused. France cut off the fresh water supply and three days later, Monaco capitulated. Today, French citizens in Monaco are taxed as if it were still part of France. The French government also nominates the principal minister of the Monaco government. Monaco has less independence than meets the eye.[7]

The point is that there is no iron curtain that descends over the offshore world, bringing a veil of darkness over the transactions of all who invest there. As previously mentioned, the legislative initiatives of the past decade were designed to stem the tide of money laundering and illicit financial activity, not to focus on the legitimate investor or business person. Therefore, the best counsel is to follow the rules. The truth is that secrecy is more often than not compromised by the individuals themselves who have gone through the process of going offshore. I was playing golf with a client who was visiting me in Nassau some time ago when we happened on a tee box behind four Canadians. After the usual pleasantries, we all started talking and the foursome told us the real reason for their trip. Recently, they had jointly established an offshore company to which they would be transferring assets for retirement and estate planning purposes. Curious, I asked for more details and was somewhat perplexed not only by their indiscretion but also by the substance of what I was told. Their method of transferring assets appeared to me to be as questionable as their choice of investments, which were largely complex financial instruments they wouldn't even consider looking at back home. The costs they alluded to seemed out of line and their understanding of how the arrangement would work in practice was sketchy. Even their choice of structure was inadequate for their overall game plan. After the bells had gone off, I saw the chance for a little fun and instruction. Their faces became horror-stricken when I told them I was actually from Revenue Canada in the Bahamas on holiday. But their shock turned to laughter when I admitted to pulling their legs.

As the laughter subsided, however, I suggested that they consider the error of their ways. They had committed one of the cardinal sins of offshore investing—romanticizing their financial affairs. Their specific mistakes were obvious: the reasons for pooling their assets hadn't been well thought out (in fact, they mistakenly thought it would be more economical to consolidate their affairs under one structure); they had failed to consider their potential tax liability, both current and future; more importantly, their choice of investments wouldn't pass the prudent investor rule and the estate and beneficiary issues they would be saddled with if one or all passed away had not been clearly defined. But their biggest mistake was the most fundamental of all: they weren't really sure why they were investing offshore in the first place. One of them had the idea and the rest followed. The blind leading the blind.

Within the offshore world, no two jurisdictions are precisely the same. To begin, some are actually high-tax, some low-tax, and some no-tax. Some have tax treaties with Canada and some do not. In the Caribbean, many jurisdictions play follow the leader, as one island introduces new legislation and the rest follow suit shortly thereafter, sometimes with little regard to the actual merit of the legislation being copied. In addition, every jurisdiction differentiates itself with regard to its capabilities. Bermuda is known for its world-class lawyers; Switzerland for its world-class bankers. Many jurisdictions have multiple capabilities or are considered generalists. Some jurisdictions that fall into this category are the Bahamas, the Cayman Islands and the Isle of Man.

The forty or so jurisdictions shown in the table "Global Offshore Jurisdictions" are most commonly associated with what investors mean by offshore. As little as five years ago, many people would choose one jurisdiction in which and from which to conduct all their international affairs. But today, particularly with the advent of high-tech communications, you can easily make use of multiple jurisdictions. For instance, many offshore players use what they perceive to be the best banking jurisdiction, while their business is located in a jurisdiction most suited for their commercial purposes, and still other jurisdictions are utilized for trust and investment needs. See the table "Trust and Corporate Structures Available in Selected Offshore Jurisdictions."

There's also a newcomer on the offshore horizon. The Internet is proving to be an extremely efficient as well as an increasingly viable medium in which to conduct international business. In the very short four or five years since the Internet has gained public acceptance, it has become an essential conduit for information and an alternative to traditional means of conducting commerce. With the rise of international Web banking, brokerage and mutual funds, the Internet may become the ultimate offshore jurisdiction in its own right in the very near future.

Global Offshore Jurisdictions

Jurisdiction	Location	Legal System	Size/ Resources	Rating (1-10; 1= excellent)
Alderney	English Channel	French/English	Very small	10
Andorra	Spain/France	French/Spanish	Very small	10
Antigua	West Indies	English	Small	9
Anguilla	West Indies	English	Small	6
Aruba (Dutch Antilles)	West Indies	Dutch	Small	7
Bahamas	West Indies	English	Medium	2
Barbados	West Indies	English	Small	3
Belize	Central America	English	Very small	9
Bermuda	Atlantic	English	Medium	3
British Virgin Islands	West Indies	English	Medium	10
Campione	Italy/Switzerland	Italian	Very small	10
Cayman Islands	West Indies	English	Large	1
Cook Islands	South Pacific	English	Small	3
Curacao (Dutch Antilles)	West Indies	Dutch	Medium	2
Cyprus	E. Mediterranean	English	Large	1
Guernsey	English Channel	English	Medium	3
Gibraltar	W. Mediterranean	English	Small	5
Hong Kong	Far East	English	Very large	1+
Isle of Man	Irish Sea	English	Large	3
Ireland	West. Europe	English	Very large	1+
Jersey	English Channel	French/English	Large	1
Lebanon	E. Mediterranean	French	Small	10
Liberia	West Africa	U.S.	Very small	9
Labuan	Far East	English	Small	3
Liechtenstein	Austria/Switz.	German	Medium	3
Luxembourg	West Europe	French	Large	1
Madeira	Atlantic	Portuguese	Small	6
Malta	Mid. Mediterranean	Italian/English	Medium	4
Mauritius	Indian Ocean	French/English	Small	4
Monaco	W. Mediterranean	French	Small	2

Global Offshore Jurisdictions continued

Jurisdiction	Location	Legal System	Size/ Resources	Rating (1-10; 1= excellent)
Nevis	West Indies	English	Very small	8
Niue	South Pacific	English	Very small	8
Panama	Central America	Spanish/U.S.	Large	3
Seychelles	Indian Ocean	French/English	Very small	9
St. Vincent	Caribbean	English	Small	7
Singapore	Far East	English	Large	2
Switzerland	Mid. Europe	French German	Very large	1
Turks & Caicos	West Indies	English	Very small	3
United Kingdom				
England	British Isles	English	Very large	1
Scotland	British Isles	Scottish	Very large	1
Uruguay	South America	Spanish	Medium	9
U.S. Virgin Islands	West Indies	U.S.	small	7
Vanuatu	Mid. Pacific	French/English	Small	6
Western Samoa	South Pacific	English	Small	6

Charles Cain, "Introduction to Offshore Jurisdictions and Concepts"

Trust and Corporate Structures Available in Selected Offshore Jurisdictions[8]

	Primary Uses	Offshore Trust Jurisdiction	International Business Companies (IBCs)	Asset Protection Trusts (APTs)
Alderney	General	No	No	No
Andorra	Residence only	No	No	No
Antigua	General	Yes	No	Yes
Anguilla	General	Yes	Yes	Yes
Aruba	Treaty	No	No	No
Bahamas	General, trusts, companies	Yes	Yes	Yes
Barbados	General	Yes	Yes	Yes
Belize	General	Yes	Yes	Yes
Bermuda	Insurance, ships, general	Yes	Yes	No
British Virgin Islands	Companies, general	Yes	Yes	Yes
Campione	Residence only	No	No	No
Cayman Islands	General, banking, insurance	Yes	Yes	Yes
Cook Islands	APTs	Yes	Yes	Yes
Curacao	Treaty	No	No	No
Cyprus	Treaty, ships, general	Yes	Yes	No
Guernsey	Insurance, general	Yes	No	No
Gibraltar	General	Yes	Yes	No
Hong Kong	Trade, general	Yes	No	No
Isle of Man	Insurance, ships, general	Yes	Perhaps	No

Structures Available in Selected Offshore Jurisdictions continued

	Primary Uses	Offshore Trust Jurisdiction	International Business Companies (IBCs)	Asset Protection Trusts (APTs)
Ireland	Freeport, treaty, companies	Yes	No	No
Jersey	Banking, general	Yes	No	No
Lebanon	Banking	No	No	No
Liberia	Companies, ships	No	No	No
Labuan	Treaty, general	Yes	No	Yes
Liechtenstein	Trusts, companies	Yes	No	No
Luxembourg	Investment, banking	No	No	No
Madeira	Trade, companies	No	No	No
Malta	Trade, banking	Yes	No	No
Mauritius	Treaty, general	Yes	Yes	Yes
Monaco	Residence, admin.	No	No	No
Nevis	General	Yes	Yes	Yes
Niue	Companies	Yes	Yes	Yes
Panama	Companies, Ships, general	No	No	No
Seychelles	General	Yes	No	No
St. Vincent	General	Yes	Yes	Yes
Singapore	Trade, treaty, general	Yes	No	No
Switzerland	Banking, investment, ins.	No	No	No
Turks & Caicos	Companies	Yes	Yes	Yes
United Kingdom				
England	Residence	No	No	No
Scotland	Residence	No	No	No
Uruguay	Treaty, companies	No	No	No
U.S. Virgin Islands		No	No	No
Vanuatu	General	No	No	No
Western Samoa	Companies	Yes	Yes	Yes

Charles Cain, "Introduction to Offshore Jurisdictions and Concepts"

CHAPTER 3

who should CONSIDER OFFSHORE?

A man's treatment of money is the most decisive test of his character—how he makes it and how he spends it.

—JAMES MOFFAT

Who should consider offshore? This question is as involved as why offshore, again for all the same reasons.

But there are certain baseline criteria, if you will, for admittance to the offshore club. If the majority of your income is required to support your lifestyle, you will have to consider your options carefully. As a rule, $150,000 of non-lifestyle assets is the minimum starting point. What I mean by "non-lifestyle" is that your house is paid off or very nearly so, you are able to contribute the maximum each year to your RRSP and you are otherwise fully invested outside of any registered plan (pension, deferred profit sharing or whatever). If that is the case and you still have $150,000 of investable assets which you wish to diversify internationally, you may want to consider your basic offshore options: a straight investment account, an asset protection structure or an estate plan, which would incorporate one or two structures. The other primary alternative is establishing a business venture or becoming involved with the international subsidiary of an existing company. For instance, franchising is becoming a popular means of establishing a presence in an offshore jurisdiction.

The important thing to realize is that the offshore advantage is no longer limited to the idle rich or swashbuckling international financier and entrepreneur. There are now virtually as many business and investment opportunities offshore as there are onshore. The question, of course, is which best (read most honestly) suits your needs.

Let's consider your investment options first. According to the *Micropal Guide to Offshore Investment Funds,* there are over 5,500 funds registered offshore. You'll find anything from Aggressive Equity to International Money Markets and every conceivable asset class and currency denomination in between. For yield-starved Canadian investors, there is hope, since the top ten offshore money market funds in the *Micropal Guide* had an average return of 17.28% for 1996. That's right, money market! A word of explanation is in order.

Many international money market managers do more than simply invest in the government Treasury bills of one country or another. Instead, they are globally focused, taking advantage of other higher-yielding, short-term debt instruments such as banker's acceptances or commercial paper, and will even play the currencies. A small portion of large-cap, blue chip equities with attractive dividend yields is also occasionally included in such money market portfolios. While this type of money market fund assumes more risk than the traditional Treasury bill funds familiar to most Canadians, such risk will be well below that of a pure "naked long" equity fund, the only other game in town for yield/return-starved investors. For the fixed-income investor, retiree or even expatriate Canadian, many yield-enhanced options are available offshore that are quite a bit more attractive than the domestic crop of fixed-income investments currently available. So offshore advantage #1 is access to a much greater universe of investment choices and superior risk-adjusted return opportunities.

But there is something else to consider in this equation: purchasing power parity.

Much ink has been spent on the topic of purchasing power parity—in the case of Canada, rightly so. Our ability as individuals to venture forth in the world with the loonie in our back pockets has been severely hampered by its relative weakness over the past few years. This is why offshore money market funds as well as many of the mixed and fixed-income funds available offshore are useful tools of diversification for Canadian dollar-based investors. These funds allow you to maintain a fixed income orientation in your portfolio while preserving your global purchasing power by diversifying away from Canadian dollar exposure. In addition, offshore money market funds are truly diversified by country (that is, they are frequently weighted on the basis of comparative GDP) as well as by currency, so that their returns are not as impacted by country-specific interest rate movements as domestic funds are.

All Aboard the Global Currency Express

In case you haven't noticed, the cost of a European vacation funded with Canadian dollars has virtually doubled in the past two years (currently, £1 = approximately C$2.45). Similarly, cross-border shopping is no longer a problem for the Canadian government, as there are fewer bargains to be found across the world's longest undefended border. For many people, summer vacations are now a matter of rediscovering Canada and all the wonders therein until such time as venturing beyond their borders becomes a less prohibitively expensive proposition.

In reality, the Canadian dollar has been weak compared to the currencies of the G7 nations for quite some time, a combination of export-dominated industrial planning and simple benign neglect. In fact, far too many pundits and policymakers are of the opinion that a weak Canadian dollar is actually good for the Canadian economy. The steroid effect of a cheap dollar in world export markets, while beneficial for trade up to a point, has masked productivity problems at home; national wealth, as measured by per capita GDP growth, has suffered as a result. The cheap loonie isn't doing any of us any good.

Let's revert to an Economics 101 example: a Canadian multinational company sells its products around the world. The currency with which it buys raw materials and pays for production and labour costs is Canadian dollars. However, receivables from sales come in a variety of currencies besides dollars, including yen, pounds, DM, etc. The multinational company, in order to remain competitive, cannot change the prices on its products every day. But the values of currencies change every day. If the Canadian dollar appreciates, our Canadian multinational will start to generate losses, as its foreign-denominated receivables will buy fewer Canadian dollars. Conversely, if the Canadian dollar weakens (as it has), our Canadian multinational will make profits as those receivables can now buy more Canadian dollars. In this scenario, the company can cut prices to become more competitive.

But a weak currency is a double-edged sword. Exporters and multinationals favour a weak currency since labour, materials and manufacturing are a bargain in comparison to the revenue generated by selling products internationally. Central banks, on the other hand, favour a stronger currency in order to achieve monetary stability. Canadian companies not only have to compete globally with their products and services; pricing is also a central factor from a potential customer's perspective. Therefore, if a Canadian company gets into a price war with an American or European competitor and the Canadian dollar starts to strengthen, the Canadian company's profit margins could be eroded very quickly as prices are dropped to attract customers. This is why multinational corporations and central banks maintain foreign reserves within their respective treasuries. By doing so, they can make use of marks, pounds or yen if as and when needed in order to protect their financial position or offset potential losses.

The reason I am focusing on this is that currency exposure must always be a consideration when individuals consider venturing offshore. Currency rates can severely affect not only large international corporations but private individuals as well. Many (if not most) international mutual funds, investment companies and financial institutions deal primarily in U.S. dollars or other major currencies, but certainly not in Canadian dollars. This puts Canadian offshore investors at an immediate disadvantage, but not if their objectives are long-term. Consider taking that portion of your assets earmarked for offshore and converting it to U.S. dollars now (yes, even at these unattractive rates) and subsequently investing in a series of offshore money market and fixed-income investments as described above. Those U.S. dollars will effectively create a hedge for your domestic savings and investments. When it comes time to make use of these funds internationally (for travel, purchasing a retirement residence or whatever), the value of the Canadian dollar will no longer be a factor. If you choose to repatriate these assets to Canada, you will more likely than not be repatriating more (even after taxes) than if you had left the assets to work for you in Canada in Canadian dollars over that same period.

No one can predict the direction of the Canadian dollar, short or long term. The international currency markets are open 24 hours a day, virtually seven days a week. The power of the central banks is limited even when it comes to supporting their own domestic currencies. For example, if all the central banks of the industrialized world decided to support only one major currency for one day, in a matter of hours they would have depleted all their foreign reserves. The only real weapon in the arsenal of the central banks is their power over short-term interest rates, which is entirely relative to each particular country's strength, stability and reputation as being fiscally and monetarily responsible (for instance, when Russia raised its short-term interest rates to 150%, how many fixed-income investors jumped to participate in that opportunity? Answer: only the brave.)

In May 1997, the Governor of the Bank of Canada, Gordon Thiessen, made an announcement to the effect that the central bank would not raise domestic interest rates for a period of six months. Immediately afterwards, the Canadian dollar lost even more ground, which clearly demonstrated that his pronouncement was and is pure fantasy. Imagine a fifty-cent dollar. Canada would effectively become a ward of the International Monetary Fund. The truth is that Canada has little control over its interest rates. If the U.S. central bank decides to raise rates, thereby making fixed-income securities and investments denominated in U.S. currency in particular more attractive, Canada has to follow in lock-step just to maintain the value of the Canadian dollar. The alternative is to suffer the consequences, as has been the case in 1997–98. National sovereignty may be defined in many ways, but it certainly cannot be said to exist when the external value of a country's currency is determined by caprice.

Cover Your Assets

Protecting the purchasing power parity of your dollars is one important aspect of offshore; another is creditor protection. Creditor protection from frivolous lawsuits, business partners, spouses, family and the like is an area of offshore that has been overlooked by many Canadians mainly because frivolous civil lawsuits and their attendant astronomical awards have been a phenomenon usually associated with south of the border. But Canada is slowly but surely becoming a litigious society as well. Professionals are increasingly at risk from frivolous lawsuits; doctors, lawyers, investment professionals and business owners in particular can all make use of the creditor protection component of offshore planning as an additional form of liability insurance.

By securing a percentage of your overall assets offshore through the use of an asset or creditor protection structure, you can effectively render those assets free from attack by potential creditors. Many offshore jurisdictions have hopped onto the creditor protection bandwagon in recent years. This development has been a direct result of the huge awards sometimes handed down by juries in U.S. civil cases. The Cook Islands, for example, have gone out of their way to facilitate the protection of private assets for U.S. citizens through what has been described as ineptly drafted legislation. Unfortunately, there is often no clear line between establishing a trust to provide protection against possible, but not yet identified, creditors and the use of trusts in an attempt to defraud existing creditors or creditors whose claims can be reasonably anticipated.[9]

I cannot tell you how many times I have received phone calls from potential clients telling me that they need an asset protection trust immediately because they are getting divorced and want to protect their assets from their soon-to-be-ex-spouse. I tell them that unfortunately they should have considered an asset protection trust two years earlier or, as a lawyer friend of mine is fond of saying, "You should have thought about this at the altar as opposed to at your lawyer's." Asset protection trusts (APT) have what is usually referred to as a *window of opportunity.*

Essentially this means that even after the APT is established, potential creditors have an opportunity to put forth their claims. In the Bahamas, the "window" is two years to determine if the settlor (the person establishing the trust) is doing so to knowingly defraud potential creditors. In matrimonial affairs, an APT can be considered the ultimate prenuptial agreement. By securing a portion of your assets in an APT while you are still single, you will be able to enjoy them after the war. Let your spouse keep the Sony. A word of caution about APTs, however, is included in Chapter 7, "To Trust or Not to Trust."

Much hype has also been generated with regard to attempts by individuals and businesses to forgo or forget the taxman in their plans to move assets and property offshore. If you are an independent business owner or professional, the taxman is already a "partner" in your affairs. Any material changes to your business, such as changing its ownership structure, moving liquid assets, declaring large dividends, etc., are duly noted by your "partner" come tax time. More liabilities are created domestically every year by individuals and businesses who forgo professional advice and adopt the "do it yourself" method of tax planning. They mistakenly or creatively omit some investment income, inadvertently take a deduction they shouldn't or declare the dog and cat as dependents and the boat as an office. The Canadian *Income Tax Act* is enormous and, rightly or wrongly, growing still. Visit Revenue Canada's Web site (www.rc.gc.ca) and take some time to peruse the various sections and subsections available online. You will be surprised and/or saddened by its enormity.

I once spoke at a financial management seminar for doctors and was extolling the virtues of domestic mutual fund investments and RRSP planning in company with a qualified financial planner and investment advisor. During the Q&A session, one of the specialists asked why he should use an advisor when he could take the information provided and "do it himself" without incurring the costs of an advisor's fee. I politely asked the good doctor how many hours a day he worked, at which he sat back with an exasperated look on his face and said, "26 hours a day." I then asked how much time he actually devoted to the analysis and allocation of investments for both his investment accounts. "Not enough," was the response. I also asked how his respective portfolios had fared in terms of performance for the 12 previous months. "Could've been better," was the response.

After the seminar the specialist and I spoke at length about his investments and his overall performance, with which he was none too pleased. Unfortunately, he still did not see the advantage of paying someone for doing something he felt he could do himself. I dug a little deeper and found out that his investment portfolios were consistently underperforming and by a rather wide margin. I bluntly told him, "You have paid more in sub-par performance over the past 12 months than the fees associated with receiving the information, advice and services of a qualified advisor." The moral of this story is that too many of these "do it yourselfers" can't see the logic of spending money on something they think they can do themselves, whether it's filing taxes, financial planning or investment management. But they pay the price in the end. It's a good thing that people in the investment business generally have the good sense to refrain from performing minor surgery on themselves. The reality is that professional accountants and investment advisors, both domestically and offshore, are readily available regardless of an individual's net worth, business acumen or investment experience. Use them.

Exploding the E-Myth

A friend of mine, who after many years of hard work has a successful and profitable self-owned business, asked me to refer him to an advisor. I asked him what type of advisor he needed: accountant, investment advisor, business consultant or financial planner. He looked at me rather perplexed and said, "All of the above." We sat down over a period of two days and reviewed his business and personal finances. During this examination, he admitted that he was in the do-it-yourself category and had probably paid too much tax on his business and consequently his personal affairs over the years. He knew he had a problem and initially didn't want to complicate it further by seeking out the proper advice, but the business was doing well and he didn't want to end up with tax or cash flow problems down the road.

This situation is all too familiar to many people. Starting a business is one of the most rewarding experiences in life as well as among the more stressful. Should I start a business or buy one? How do I come up with the right idea? Will my idea work? Can this idea be turned into a viable business? How much money do I need—and where do I get it? These are just some of the many questions business owners and entrepreneurs ask themselves when starting out. Questions concerning who will do the books, marketing, finance, etc. are usually not part of the initial process. That's unfortunate, since so many great ideas and businesses fail or never even make it off the ground because of these oversights.

Michael E. Gerber, author of *The E-Myth Revisited*, examines the pros and cons of entrepreneurial pursuits and entrepreneurs themselves; he provides some very good insights for anyone who has thought of starting a business or for individuals who are in business for themselves. The E-Myth is defined as "a romantic belief that small businesses are started by entrepreneurs, when, in fact, most are not." Gerber contends that technicians, people who have a certain skill set or know how to do something in particular, start most businesses. Gerber also points out that people who go into business on their own have to be a kind of Trinity or three people in one: the Entrepreneur, the Manager and the Technician. He also says quite succinctly, "The problem with most failing businesses I've encountered is not that their owners don't know enough about finance, marketing, management and operations—they don't, but those things are easy enough to learn—but that they spend their time and energy defending what they know."

I gave Gerber's book to my friend and told him to ask himself what he liked most and least about his business. He took one of Gerber's key suggestions to heart: listing those duties and/or obligations that he disliked or did not know how to do, and instead of taking the time to learn and perform them personally, subcontract them. Sounds simple enough, but it took him nearly 16 months to establish outsourcing relationships he felt comfortable with. Why? "Would you give your child over to the first babysitter that walked through your door?" was his response. And he's right. What is important is that your advisors "fit." By that I mean that you are comfortable with and confident in your advisor's experience, personality and abilities and that he or she is fundamentally mindful of your company (or baby if you like). More importantly, you should make the effort to understand—if not actually take care of—everything that your advisors are doing on your behalf. After all, it's your life and livelihood they are advising you on.

If Gerber's thesis is right, you may only be the "technician," but it is after all your company. Don't be afraid to ask questions or request clarification on issues. By having a better understanding of your business and financial situation, you make easier not only your own life but the lives of your advisors as well. My friend has since recruited his accountant into his firm full-time and is preparing to do the same with his business consultant. These same advisors are now doing a feasibility study as to the benefits of expanding the business internationally. What did Samuel Johnson say about the man who tended to his own health having a fool for a doctor?

The Business Case for Offshore

Offshore investment is going through what I would term a renaissance, and the number of new businesses being formed or relocated to offshore jurisdictions is multiplying. Here is something I heard at a conference not too long ago: "If Microsoft was formed today, the company and Bill [Gates] would probably be offshore."

This is not as far-fetched as you might imagine. Many of today's emerging high-tech companies are increasingly looking offshore for business solutions and opportunities. Some of these companies are tax-motivated, while increasing regulatory restraints at home motivate others. There are, however, some very sound business reasons for looking to establish or move your company's base of operations to a more favourable jurisdiction. As a case in point, consider Doug Mellinger and his custom software engineering firm, PRT Barbados. His story and his company were recently featured both in *INC.* magazine and a CNN profile. Doug Mellinger's company designs custom software for some of the largest financial institutions in the world, including J. P. Morgan of New York and other illustrious banking names.

Mellinger faced any number of obstacles in the initial establishment of his company in the United States. The demand for software engineers in Silicon Valley has virtually outstripped the available supply. This has resulted in skyrocketing salaries for qualified and available engineers, making employment financially prohibitive for many companies. Top programmers are always being confronted with better offers, or, worse, taking mountain biking sabbaticals. PRT had grown to $8 million in sales through its unique strategy of applying programmers to specific client tasks as opposed to offering "one size fits all" products. In doing so, Mellinger had begun to recruit programmers who, even as far back as 1991, came from as far away as India. In this process, he also spent years dealing with mountains of bureaucratic red tape trying to set up a subsidiary in India, only to watch it come to nothing. The engineers in India were more than skilled, but his labour-deprived company could not bring this needed talent into the United States because of immigration restrictions; equally, he couldn't tap overseas talent on the ground because of a variety of regulatory and other obstacles in those countries. This could be termed onshore checkmate.

So Mellinger conceived a revolutionary solution. He decided that he would "create" a country, a country where the company, its programmers and clients would want to come, stay, work freely and develop and write what he liked to term "killer code," a sort of Delphic oracle for software development. That country would have to possess a welcoming environment conducive to better living and doing better business. In the end, instead of doing a pure Robinson Crusoe play, Mellinger established a partnership with Barbados in the southern Caribbean. In exchange for allowing PRT to establish itself and bring in the necessary programmers and personnel, PRT would assist the government of Barbados in leapfrogging the industrial stage of economic development into a global, technology-based, knowledge-driven future. True to their word, PRT is currently working with the local education system and with the utility and public works ministries to develop much-needed infrastructure.

This partnership illustrates what can be accomplished when both private and public sectors of the economy come together. Far from being perceived as a benevolent or semi-charitable organization, PRT is succeeding in a very competitive global environment even while not being located in a major centre. The other surprising aspect of PRT's culture is the company's retention of valued programmers. While working for a company located in Barbados is a pleasant enough prospect, PRT goes even further in making employees a part of the company, a family if you will. Mellinger always knew that PRT would have to provide the basics of life for his employees. But what he did that may have been somewhat unexpected was create "the life." Housing, transportation, healthcare, insurance, legal concerns, banking affairs, virtually everything is taken care of. From the moment newcomers arrive on the island, they are met at the airport, relieved of their baggage, guided through immigration, given a cash advance and then chauffeured to their freshly prepared house where they are met with greetings and social invitations from neighbours and colleagues. Equally impressive is the refrigerator, stocked with all of the newcomer's favourite foods and refreshments. Newcomers always make a point of mentioning "the fridge." Later on, employees' bills are paid. They get free transportation. Their savings pile up in the bank, even though their salaries are less than what they could make in a market like New York or Los Angeles.

"I don't want them to have to think about anything but having fun and writing killer code," says Mellinger. His gamble on creating a virtual country is paying off. In the past two years, more than 300 software engineers have immigrated to Barbados from all over the world. Would-be PRT programmers undergo an extensive interview and testing process. The enterprise has been so successful at attracting and keeping engineers that Barbados is now a community to which not many are any longer getting invitations.

With PRT's success—and because client expectations are being exceeded—the company is receiving work and requests for upper-echelon projects. Mellinger and his colleagues have created something from nothing and in the meantime established a partnership where all parties involved come out ahead. PRT Barbados was heading toward a $19 million budgeted year in 1997, but the company would eventually achieve $62 million in sales in 1997, while an initial public offering would finance a near-doubling of the company's sales to $120 million in 1998.

Mellinger's ability to look beyond his current situation, identify the needs of his industry and enlist the help of the necessary players to assist in creating a "country" are a wonderful example of what can be achieved in an offshore environment. Doug Mellinger refers to his company as the "antiheroic company." He doesn't ask "how" to solve a problem, he asks "who" can solve it. This gives everyone within the organization the opportunity to have an impact on the direction and success of the company. This shared commitment philosophy is also what helped PRT establish itself in a foreign country with the full blessing and assistance of the government and community.[10]

Many of the business owners I have talked to are looking for situations similar to PRT's. This is where your choice of offshore advisors and/or partners becomes crucial. They should first of all understand where you are coming from and then assist you in understanding what it is that they can do for you, and what is expected of you if you choose to work within their jurisdiction. Your sensitivity to their jurisdiction's political, social and economic requisites cannot be underestimated. Beyond immediate profits and get-rich-quick schemes, offshore centres are looking for long-term participation in their economies and give preference to companies that establish themselves with a view to giving something back.

As the popularity of offshore and international business continues, many centres are looking for companies and partnerships such as the PRT example to move forward in the global marketplace. Caribbean offshore centres cannot and will not be able to survive on tourism and banking alone; many of the more progressive jurisdictions have already come to this realization. The Bahamas, for example, has built a solid reputation in the banking and trust business, but has fallen behind in the establishment of an investment management community (along with full-service brokerage and independent broker/dealers). The government and financial community recognize this and are working to establish the necessary legislation and infrastructure to add more of a knowledge base, not just transactional proficiency, to this facet of its domestic economy. The ability of Caribbean offshore jurisdictions to leapfrog into the global technology and information-based economy will determine which jurisdictions succeed and which will not. I expect that our list of forty or so key offshore jurisdictions will expand over the coming years as demand for business and tax-friendly environments grows. So who should consider business offshore? Anyone with the drive, spirit, vision and determination of a Doug Mellinger. Surprisingly, there are quite a few individuals like him around.

CHAPTER 4

taxation
THE MOTIVATING FACTOR THAT CAN'T BE

What that April his shoures soor

Returns of total income dooth outpoor,

On whiche on peyne of been o'erheigh assessed

Ech must reveel of what he is possessed,

Al men bethinkle hem what they can abate,

And how perchaunce they maybe reduce the rate.

Tis hard to saye if skill more gretely wax

In earning income or avoyding tax.

—Geoffrey Chaucer, formerly H. M. Comptroller of Customs on wool, skin and leather for the Port of London, 1374 and Comptroller of Petty Customs, 1382

I frequently meet people who are armed with a mission and absolute sense of purpose: they are quite frankly teed off and want to do nothing more than get as much of their money out of Canada as quickly as possible, consequences be damned. "I make $200K a year. After taxes, I'm left with less than $100K; converting that into real money—U.S. dollars—and I have about US$68K left. And for what do I pay so much in taxes? The government is defaulting on its healthcare promises, education costs are spiraling upwards and I can't possibly save fast enough because the government is there with its hand out the moment I profit from any investments I make."

This is a compendium of the complaints I hear all too often. What's more, what they are saying is true. Canada's highest marginal tax rate of 52% kicks in at the $65,000 level of earned income, while in the United States the highest marginal rate of 40% kicks in at approximately US$350,000. Is it any wonder that many Canadians have been and will continue to seek relief in any way they can in order to spread their financial wings? Historically, people haven't minded paying taxes as long as the level of taxation is perceived to be fair. But fair is a word that is rarely uttered by Canadians when it comes to taxation.

NO MAN IN THIS COUNTRY IS UNDER THE SMALLEST OBLIGATION, MORAL OR OTHER, SO TO ARRANGE HIS LEGAL RELATIONS TO HIS BUSINESS OR PROPERTY, AS TO ENABLE THE INLAND REVENUE TO PUT THE LARGEST SHOVEL INTO HIS STORES.

—Scottish High Court Justice Lord Clyde (1848)

Taxes, Taxes Everywhere and No Relief In Sight

The Government of Canada has been faced with the daunting task of stemming the flow of funds from Canada to offshore jurisdictions over the past thirty years. Ottawa's response has been to spawn rather draconian legislation as well as some horrific thinking. The most recent piece of legislation, Bill C-92, which contains the offshore disclosure rules, was passed very quietly and unceremoniously on April 25, 1997 (the offshore disclosure rules were shelved for review, but will probably be enforced for the 1999 taxation year). This bill took much criticism throughout its readings in Parliament and subsequent passing into law. For example, representatives of Vancouver's business community warned that the legislation would seriously impact the investment decision-making process of the Asian-Canadian community, while the Vancouver real estate board stated that it would drastically depress the Vancouver-area housing market. Since timing is everything, it is interesting to note that, while this legislation was being passed, 10,000 miles away across the Pacific the Asian crisis was beginning to unfold. The spectre of the new disclosure legislation and concurrently the bargain basement prices afforded by a 60% depreciation in some Asian currencies made the flight of capital and people from the Vancouver area inevitable.

The offshore disclosure rules are not alone in their impact on potential foreign investment in Canada. Individuals once drawn to establishing residency or undertaking commerce in this country will now consider other jurisdictions that offer a more favourable business environment and a fairer system of taxation. Remember that Canada originally invited wealthy individuals to enter its borders under the Immigrant Investor Program, which began in the 1980s. But now, when these individuals are ensconced as part of the Canadian mosaic, running businesses and creating jobs, the federal government has firmly closed the door by informing them that they must henceforth disclose all foreign assets or face stiff penalties (two minutes for succeeding, eh?).

Many entrepreneurs who entered Canada under the Immigrant Investor Program already pay taxes on their property, businesses or investments in their home jurisdictions and view this legislation as nothing more than an embryonic dual taxation system. This type of legislation should be an election issue, but many have already voted on it—with their feet. In essence, Canada is now biting the hand that feeds it, while countries such as New Zealand and Australia have declared that they are open for business to Asian investors. Canada has once again stubbed its toes on the road to global competitiveness by effectively alienating some of the world's most innovative, independently wealthy individuals, those autonomous entrepreneurs I referred to at the beginning of this book, the same people every other developing or developed nation is vying to attract. Canada cannot stand on its laurels as being one of the best, if not the best, places to live if success is to be considered a four-letter word.

But before we continue, let's get something straight. The ideas and information contained in this book are not the ramblings of some unpatriotic, ex-resident Canadian who from his new home in the islands is screaming that the grass is greener. The grass is not greener. My wife and I often discuss the many conveniences, or perhaps they should be called luxuries, we now have to do without, such as fully stocked grocery stores and President's Choice products. Or utilities that work properly when you finally have them installed. Or dirt in the streets and confusion at the airport. We also discuss some of the things we miss most about Canada: the autumn, friends and family. Few, if any, offshore books and periodicals discuss the sacrifices necessary in becoming non-resident, since taxation is usually their sole focus. But they do exist.

Some people warm to the idea of living and working in different environments, while others do not or cannot. But patriotism has little if anything to do with the subjects discussed herein. In fact, on the issue of patriotism, why spend your tax dollars on a Heritage Ministry to boost patriotism and revive Canadian identity, when a significant cut in taxes or a favourable rebalancing of the levels at which marginal tax rates kick in would have Canadians swinging and shouting from the rafters since their increased disposable income would make them feel a lot better about their choice of nationality? Give people an incentive to invest in their country without fear of excessive taxation and watch the Canadian identity, to say nothing of the domestic economy, regain lost ground. This would be a little more exciting and far more inclusive of the voting public than watching Sheila Copps distribute flags.

At the far right of the political spectrum in North America is the idea of having complete and unfettered capitalism with governments being relegated to the roles of limited civil administration and national defense. But even Adam Smith, the Scottish economist and author of *Wealth of Nations*, published in 1776 and handbook of the right wing, made disparaging comments with regard to unfettered capitalism and the eventual social and economic ills it would envelop society in. As always, the truth is probably somewhere in between.

VERY HIGH LEVELS OF TAXATION HAVE RESULTED IN EXTENSIVE ILLEGAL TAX EVASION AND LEGAL TAX AVOIDANCE. DIFFICULT TO DRAW THE LINE.

—V. A. Ladd, Commissioner of Inland Revenue for Hong Kong (1979–1986), who coined the term "avoision"

I'm Mad as Hell and I'm Not Going to Take It Anymore

Regardless of politics, many Canadians are taking matters into their own hands with the refrain from the Academy-Award-winning film *Network* in mind. Because an environment of fear and anxiety has arisen among taxpayers, more than a few have adopted a rather cavalier attitude with regard to moving their personal assets outside the Canadian taxation system. A word of advice: move carefully when considering any offshore opportunity. Many investment options are intriguing, but more often than not they lack the substance that should be demanded by Canadian investors. It's not enough to simply exploit a soon-to-be-closed loophole or accept a combination of bad advice and bad planning that could create a liability for yourself or your beneficiaries.

Consider the following reasonably recent news item:

> OTTAWA, March 18, 1997—Revenue Canada today reported that Bill Rogers of Vancouver, British Columbia and Ken Rogers of Kelowna, British Columbia, both formerly of Calgary, Alberta, were each sentenced to two years less a day in jail after pleading guilty on February 5, 1997 in British Columbia provincial court to 20 charges of evading federal income taxes. Their company, Auramet International Ltd., was also fined $9,239,895.04. A Revenue Canada investigation revealed that Bill Rogers and Ken Rogers promoted the sale of units in limited partnerships during 1986 and 1987 through Auramet International Ltd. The two men were directors of the company which operated in British Columbia and Alberta. The company used offshore companies in the Netherlands Antilles and British Virgin Islands to create false expenses. This allowed investors in the limited partnerships to reduce their taxes. In addition, false entries were made in the books and records of Auramet International Ltd. so that investors could avoid paying capital gains tax. Information obtained from Curaçao, Netherlands Antilles, revealed that Bill Rogers and Ken Rogers used offshore companies to create false invoices for foreign exploration expenses. They set up a number of bank accounts at a bank at Curaçao, Netherlands Antilles and made a series of transactions which created an illusion of deposits and withdrawals in an effort to prove that the false invoices were paid. Revenue Canada will challenge non-compliance with tax laws. However, individuals who have not filed returns for previous years or who have not reported all their income can still voluntarily correct their tax affairs. The department will not penalize or prosecute them if they make a full disclosure before the department starts any action or investigations against them. These taxpayers will only have to pay the taxes owing, plus interest.[11]

Note that Revenue Canada caught these gentlemen ten years after the fact. This is what I mean by creating a potential future liability for yourself and your beneficiaries. How many investors in this little scheme had near-coronaries on hearing the news? How many more are wondering if they will have enough left for retirement and to hand over to their beneficiaries let alone be able to provide immediately for their families today. If you are looking for business opportunities offshore, this is not how to go about it. No one looks kindly on fraud and deceit, least of all the revenue authorities or staff at financial institutions, and that's how Revenue Canada was able to obtain the information they needed from Curaçao. The financial institutions involved would have been more than compliant, because they would have been happy to rid themselves of the Rogerses of this world and the liabilities they had created for them.

This sort of onshore/offshore investment scheme is all the more lamentable because legitimate business and investment opportunities do exist. If you are seriously considering any offshore investments that originate from Canada, I'd suggest that you get a second or even third opinion. Ask yourself: Why would John Smith of Anyplace, Canada be selling offshore investments to Canadian-resident taxpayers while being a resident himself? These opportunities may be legitimate, but perhaps they merit additional questioning. Professional advice is the one area that many offshore investors neglect at their peril. I'm not talking about the advice of the person selling you their products and services, but the advice of a tax professional sensitive to the issues of the resident Canadian taxpayer. Too many people seem to feel that conducting an investment program offshore is the same as onshore. "I'll simply call 1-800-NO-LOAD and my offshore investments will be a breeze." The tax and reporting issues that present themselves when Canadians venture offshore are complex, onerous and penalizing if not addressed properly. There are right now tens of thousands of Canadian-resident taxpayers under the impression that the non-resident discretionary trust they established fifteen years or so ago is free and clear of any and all reporting to the Canadian tax authorities. Unfortunately, time and circumstances have changed and now the settlor and all beneficiaries (whether they know they are beneficiaries or not) are in the position of being required to report.

The Rules—What You Need to Know

Every resident Canadian taxpayer is obligated to report all worldwide income when filing his or her annual tax return. This includes any income earned from bank accounts held abroad, offshore trusts, investment accounts and/or dividends or payments from offshore corporations. Interestingly, Canadian citizenship confers one advantage that our American cousins do not share: Canadians are taxed on the basis of residency; U.S. citizens on the basis of citizenship. That is to say, all U.S. citizens have a tax obligation to the U.S. government no matter where they may live in the world; although that obligation only kicks in after the first $70,000 of earned income, they still have to file annually just as if they were living on Main Street America even though they may now live in another country. In order for U.S. citizens to become truly tax-free, they must actually give up their citizenship and hand over their passports. The United States is one of only a handful of countries that tax individuals on this basis. Most countries tax individuals on the basis of their residency, as Canada does. But before you begin to shake your head in sympathy, wait: there has been talk of doing the same in Canada, i.e., taxing Canadians on citizenship no matter where they live. Last one out turn off the lights.

In the thousands of pages in the income and excise tax acts, finding what you need to know can be a challenging affair. I will not go into great detail, but I will point out the more relevant sections of the *Income Tax Act* that confront Canadians who are currently involved in an offshore business or investment venture, who are looking to possibly create a tax deferral on offshore assets or for anyone considering their offshore options.

The Foreign Accrual Property Income (FAPI) rules deal specifically with the issues of controlled and non-controlled foreign affiliates and how ownership, whether whole or in part, affects Canadian resident taxpayers. In other words, simply owning an international business company (IBC) that earns income through investments puts the Canadian-resident taxpayer in a reporting situation. The next section is section 94.1, the Offshore Investment Fund Property Rules, which details the type and style of investments that are both exempt and possibly non-exempt under the Act. This section, in combination with the FAPI rules, also sets out the determination process of active versus passive investment. Bill C-92, which contains the Offshore Disclosure Rules, also details the process of declaring trusts whether you are the settlor/grantor or beneficiary. This is the provision that seeks to know basically anything and everything concerning Canadian-resident taxpayers and their involvement in offshore trusts. Most importantly, the penalties for non-compliance under C-92 are very steep indeed. Finally, there's everyone's favourite piece of mysterious legislation., the General Anti-avoidance Rules or GAAR. This is as ambiguous in its wording as it is in its conception, and GAAR has yet to be tried successfully in the courts.

Essentially, what the tax rules boil down to is this. Revenue Canada, through the legislation and rules we'll briefly examine in more detail plus additional sections of the *Income Tax Act*, has rendered most structures (i.e., trusts, IBCs, etc.) transparent. This means that the tax authorities don't care about what structure you have utilized; what they want to know about you, as an individual, resident Canadian taxpayer, is where the money is located and how it is invested so that they may determine whether there is tax owing on the income from any particular scheme. But this legislation, like the Act itself, is subject to interpretation. For example, many offshore investment schemes designed for Canadians will usually have a tax opinion rendered by a reputable tax attorney available for your perusal. The purpose of this opinion is to state whether the venture is indeed tax-effective and lay out the reasoning behind its structure and tax-effectiveness. For a little comparison shopping, I have from time to time collected a number of these opinions and given them to other tax experts for their review; invariably they have stated that according to their interpretation the opinion and therefore the investment itself was not tax-effective. Interpretation and the defense of a particular interpretation are a key component to tax-effectiveness. Understanding what is and is not allowable under the Act is paramount and the responsibility of the individual making the investment. However, this entire area is highly complex and requires consultation for further clarification with a professional in the tax field as it pertains to each individual investor's circumstances.

Foreign Accrual Property Income (FAPI)

Limiting the ability of Canadians to earn tax-free, passive (i.e., investment) income offshore was the primary objective of the famous tax reform initiatives of 1972 (which brought us valuation day, among other reforms). At that time, sections 91 through 95 were introduced as part of the *Income Tax Act.* Basically these sections laid the ground rules for Canadian investors, requiring them to include in their Canadian taxable income any share of Foreign Accrual Property Income from a controlled foreign affiliate. The FAPI rules didn't actually come into effect until 1976, but by that time a number of Canadian-offered funds had been structured in such a way as to permit investors to earn income that could not be attributed to them (basically interest rollup funds), yet retain earnings so as to give rise to a capital gain and therefore take advantage of the "once upon a time" capital gains exemption. A number of funds were designed to avoid Canadian taxes altogether, which resulted in the introduction of section 94.1 in the federal budget of February 15, 1984. The FAPI rules are but one of the set of provisions laid out by Revenue Canada to ensure payment of taxes on investment income from foreign jurisdictions. You may not actually have received the income due to the fact that an offshore trust or corporation earned it; but if you meet the conditions under the rules, you will be taxable as a resident of Canada. These rules are extensive and highly complex, so I will only touch on the basics. FAPI generally applies to certain non-active investments in foreign companies that are characterized as controlled foreign affiliates. FAPI would apply if a resident Canadian taxpayer:

- Owns more than 50% of the voting stock of an issuer or fund
- Owns less than 50%, but the remaining shareholders are related parties
- Owns less than 50%, but the issuer or fund has no more than five (5) shareholders[12]

As you can see, there is little room to hide from the feds here.

Section 94.1: The Offshore Investment Fund Property Rules

The purpose of this section was to put an end to the offshore fund investments that were widely available to Canadian investors through the 1970s and early 1980s. These two-tiered or deferral/conversion funds basically deferred all income due to investors and at year-end converted such income into a separate class of shares that were then held in trust and could only be taxed on a capital gains basis. This bit of financial engineering got Revenue Canada's dander up and so the ambiguously worded section 94.1 was born. This section applies only to foreign or offshore investments that are made by Canadian-resident taxpayers. The offshore investment fund property is defined as a share of the capital stock of, interest in or debt of a "non-resident entity," where the value is attributable to "portfolio investments" and where the motivating factor in making the investment was a significant reduction or deferral of taxes. This is otherwise known as the motive or purpose test, i.e., was the motivating factor for, or purpose of, the offshore investment solely the reduction, deferral or avoidance of taxes?

The term "portfolio investments" is very broadly defined within section 94.1 and bears both scrutiny and further comment. According to Revenue Canada, to be considered an offshore investment fund property, an investment made by a Canadian resident taxpayer must reasonably be considered to derive its value primarily from portfolio investments in:

- Shares of the capital stock of a corporation or corporations
- Debt instruments or annuities
- Interests in one or more trusts, partnerships, organizations, funds or entities
- Commodities
- Real estate
- Canadian or foreign resource properties
- Currency of a country other than Canada
- Rights or options to acquire or dispose of any of the above
- Any combination of the foregoing

The word "primarily" and its interpretation by Revenue Canada are not considered definitive enough by most tax experts in the assessment of whether a particular company, corporation or investment may fall under the definition. Revenue Canada, however, stands by its use of the term and the broad meaning of "portfolio investment." Such determinations depend largely on what portfolio investment is considered to be in commercial practice by professional investors, investment managers, investment promoters and the like. But more important is how it is used in the context of the Act. Section 94.1 is regarded as an anti-avoidance provision, so Revenue Canada maintains that it is not concerned with the wide and ambiguous wording of the section. This is definitely a concern for those taxpayers who are investing offshore for the purpose of avoiding tax. As pointed out above, section 94.1 contains a very broad description of the type of investments that may be applicable under the rules. Investments such as stocks, bonds, commodities and real estate clearly fall under these rules. In fact, it is generally acknowledged that this definition would include all types of property an investor might hold. But the definition becomes ambiguous when consideration is given to certain types of newer investments and securities, such as actively traded commodity portfolios, stock index futures, synthetic debt or equity instruments and swaps. Interestingly, a number of these more innovative offshore investments, such as actively managed hedge funds and swap programs, not only deal effectively with 94.1 but also provide attractive, risk-adjusted rates of return that exceed those of similar investments available in Canada.

The motive test, which was by and large the main hurdle inherent in the section for individual taxpayers, made it extremely difficult to establish motives other than the reduction, deferral or avoidance of tax. In fact, case law in this area has already yielded the result that a taxpayer must demonstrate that in no way did the reasoning behind the investment involve the reduction of Canadian tax. Moreover, the motive test must be met for the life of the investment and not simply on acquisition. There have been, however, some breaks in terms of the interpretation of motive and some more reasonable or at least less restrictive thinking since the establishment of this section. The availability of investments otherwise not available domestically as well as investment management techniques not typically accessible to Canadian investors have merited reasonable consideration under 94.1. Reasonable would constitute examining the investment on an individual basis in order to determine whether it could be viewed somewhat more leniently in consideration of the nature of the investment opportunity as well as the risk assumed by the investor. This in turn would be weighed against any possible tax benefit that the investor could possibly receive.

Furthermore, section 94.1 does something no other similar legislation in any other jurisdiction has mandated: it attributes deemed income at a prescribed rate to the owner of an investment that qualifies as offshore investment fund property. The calculation of this imputed income is: the product of the designated cost of the investment at the end of each month and one-twelfth of the prescribed interest rate for that month. This alone has served as a major disincentive to individual investors considering offshore investments, individuals who would otherwise voluntarily and fully disclose their assets yet view the imputed income prescribed as an unnecessary additional cost. Section 94.1 effectively put an end to the wholesale abuses and widespread avoidance of taxes that preceded it. Yet the imputed income rules in the section are viewed as unfair by most sophisticated investors and their tax advisors.

Some people are still under the mistaken assumption that owning offshore investments through an IBC precludes them from worrying about the reporting requirements of section 94.1, and that therefore they are free and clear, since under FAPI, investments in controlled foreign affiliates are not included as offshore investment fund properties. Unfortunately, a rule in paragraph 95(1)(b)(ii.1) requires a controlled foreign affiliate that owns such property to include imputed income in its FAPI. If you ever think you've found a loophole on your own, think again. This ground has been well covered.[13]

Bill C-92 and the Offshore Disclosure Rules

This legislation did not introduce any new taxing provisions, but did launch far-reaching reporting requirements with respect to foreign interests held in jurisdictions outside Canada by Canadians. (See the table "Information Returns with Respect to Foreign Property.") Taxpayers with foreign affiliates will have to provide additional financial and tax information. Failure to comply with these requirements will result in the imposition of substantial penalties.

The penalties for failure to comply are steep. For example, the minimum penalty for failure to file return T1135 is $500 per month, for up to 24 months. The penalty can increase to $1,000 a month if an information return is not produced subsequent to a request made by Revenue Canada. If you then go beyond 24 months, the penalty moves up to 10% of the amount in question.[14]

The General Anti-Avoidance Rule (GAAR)

The General Anti-Avoidance Rule is intended to prevent abusive tax avoidance. Any transaction, or one that is part of a series of transactions, of which the intent is either directly or indirectly to result in a tax benefit, is considered tax-motivated and therefore comes under this rule. But what nonsense! GAAR flies in the face of the common law precept that individuals must be allowed to arrange or plan their affairs so as to attract the least amount of tax—a legitimate and accepted facet of Canadian tax law. GAAR is basically maintaining that unless a transaction has some bona fide purpose other than obtaining a tax benefit, the tax benefit obtained will be revoked. This is why we have witnessed the demise of certain limited partnership structures and flow-through share arrangements over the past decade.

Information Returns with Respect to Foreign Property

Foreign affiliates	T1134
Interests in a foreign property	T1135
Transfers and loans to a foreign trust	T1141
Distributions from a foreign trust	T1142

GAAR exemplifies the Canadian attitude toward taxation. Its wording is deliberately ambiguous, and the penalties, if they do in fact apply to any transaction that fits the GAAR profile, are such that the time, effort and money invested become a moot issue since your time, money and effort will be spent doing battle with the Revenue Canada authorities. Canada's movement in the direction of tax reform is long overdue; and it should start quickly, since many of the baby boomers who can afford to are going to be looking elsewhere to spend their retirement years. More important is the exodus of 30–40-year-olds from Canada for better opportunities as well as the wholesale recruitment of Canadian university computer and tech grads south of the border. These individuals are the prime income earners in society. History is simply repeating itself. The same outflow of 30–40-year-olds from the United Kingdom to Canada and parts north, south, east and west was at high tide during the United Kingdom's brief but damaging experiment with excessive taxation during the 1960s and 1970s. Our situation is not unique, nor do our solutions have to be unique.

CHAPTER 5

I'm leaving on a jet plane

THE NON-RESIDENCY OPTION

Non-residency is an option that many Canadians are just beginning to consider more seriously, and for myriad reasons. From a business perspective, leaving Canada can mean greater access to financing and/or venture capital, a more favourable regulatory and tax environment and access to skilled, technical or lower-cost labour. These are all attractive considerations which, coupled with government incentive programs for moving into certain jurisdictions as per the PRT Barbados example in Chapter 4, have become very appealing for Canadian and international business alike. From the individual taxpayer's perspective, however, non-residency has not been as compelling over the last thirty or so years because of the advantages of remaining a Canadian resident, such as the healthcare system, the education system, and so on. But as Bank of Montreal reminds us, the times they are a-changin'. The healthcare or "healthscare" system is now a source of fear and anxiety rather than security for Canada's rapidly aging population; at the same time, a significant proportion of the baby boomers are now empty-nesters, so education is no longer a factor for this largest individual segment of the population. In fact, the entire social safety net Canadians used to cite in justifying solidarity with Canada is no longer the magnet that keeps us grounded to the country.

For many of those who have contemplated it, the allure of offshore is emotional. How many times have you gone on vacation and said, "Let's not leave." "Wouldn't it be nice just to stay here?" "Let's throw in the towel, simplify our lives and move here." "This is the perfect retirement spot," etc., etc. A year *en Provence* perhaps? My parents have travelled quite extensively in their time and my mother always says the same thing on her return home: "Canada is a great place to live and am I happy I'm home." Non-residency would not suit my parents or thousands of Canadians like them, but this is an area of great interest for others who see the world as a much smaller place than it was thirty years ago and are weighing the pros and cons of a temporary or permanent leap to another country. I knew years before the opportunity presented itself that I wanted to travel, work and live my life in a different country, as did many of my friends and colleagues. Perhaps it is a generational issue; then again, perhaps not.

Canadians who are approaching retirement, or, better yet, retired, are examining the possibility of non-residency as well. Many are taking the "snowbird" concept of leaving Canada during the harsh winter months in favour of a better climate to new and exciting levels. Whereas in the past concerns about healthcare and health insurance presented a sizable obstacle to becoming a non-resident, solutions in the form of better, more flexible and more reasonably priced health insurance have emerged from a variety of carriers, including many Canadian insurance companies. More importantly, the realization that the net cost savings of privately funded medical insurance compared to the income tax bite that is actually funding this "free" benefit is dawning on many people. Remember that approximately 40% of your annual provincial tax bill goes to fund healthcare; in the higher tax brackets, that can be quite a sizable amount. Canadians have little experience purchasing private healthcare coverage and the types of plans and coverage options can be quite intimidating, so it should be researched with an insurance specialist. Coverage is extremely important, and it must be determined by your family needs. For example, if you were accepting a foreign posting from your employer, you would most likely be provided with the necessary coverage, but it is still always a good idea to have your plan thoroughly reviewed by external professionals as well. Depending on your global destination—and if not part of your original plan—additional coverage, say, for airlifting or evacuation in the case of serious medical emergency may be necessary. I've heard many a horror story of people standing beside their loved ones who are lying in pain on a stretcher while they try and negotiate the cost of the ambulance, plane and medical treatment associated with airlifting them to a better centre. This is not an experience anyone should have to go through when the health of a family member is at stake. On hearing one too many of these stories, my wife and I supplemented our health insurance plan and enrolled with a company that specializes in medical air services. The advent of more efficient and cheaper means of travel is a major reason why the world is a much smaller place and why people can plan for multiple trips to and from anywhere in the world, even if the purpose of the trip is life-saving, not sightseeing.

Another primary reason for renewed examination of the non-residency option is, of course, taxes. RRSPs are a great means of reducing your taxable income by maximizing your annual contributions, but the truth is that sooner or later you will be taxed on the growth of these assets at your full marginal rate. That fact combined with the old age security clawbacks, the precarious state of the Canada Pension Plan and the potential return of estate taxes have prompted many people to examine their alternatives in an attempt to put their retirement future and the future of their estate back into their own hands.

But the idea of becoming non-resident is not something to be considered lightly, and there are far more questions to be raised beyond those of a strictly financial nature. My wife and I were counselling a couple we know well about the prospects of retiring as non-residents. The husband had researched many of the jurisdictions that would meet their needs from a lifestyle as well as a tax and financial planning perspective. Ireland provided the requisite lifestyle considerations, since golf was their passion; and Ireland being a treaty country with Canada, it was possible for them to deregister their RRSPs there at a withholding tax rate of 15%, as opposed to the 25% that would have applied had they remained in Canada. Given the size of their combined RRSP, those ten percentage points were significant. But in the end, they did not choose to become non-residents, because of a number of factors, some large, some small. That's how it works. While it does wonders for the fairways, the wet, dreary Irish weather did not appeal to them, nor did the size or amenities of the houses compared to what they were accustomed to in Canada. Most importantly, they felt they would be too distant from their children and grandchildren. Continuing to look around, they checked out Barbados, another treaty country, where the climate was far better and the housing more than adequate, but the golf was not as appealing and they were still too far from family and loved ones. What they eventually settled on was downsizing to a condominium closer to their children in Canada and maintaining a vacation residence in Florida; in this way, they felt they had the best of all worlds regardless of the possible tax savings associated with becoming non-resident. Once again, this underlines the fact that tax should not and really cannot be the sole motivating factor in making decisions that ultimately affect your lifestyle. I know any number of miserable expatriates whose primary motive was tax and now spend their time pining over what they miss most about their home jurisdictions.

If, however, non-residency is an option you do find appealing, research your options thoroughly to ensure the end result is going to be a happy one. Enlist the aid of a tax expert in Canada who thoroughly understands this specialized area in order to fully appreciate what is involved. Any fees paid in the process should be viewed as insurance necessary to execute this option properly. You will most likely want to do the same in your chosen jurisdiction, since no two tax systems are identical and your new country of choice will probably have taxation issues that merit further scrutiny. A thorough examination of the country to which you wish to emigrate is paramount. Reviewing that country's tax, business and investment systems will help greatly in your decision-making process or may even prompt you to consider another jurisdiction altogether. Becoming non-resident is not simply a case of leaving Canada for more than 183 days a year and returning to the comforts of home and lifestyle in Canada for the remainder of the year.

Mention has been made of tax treaties and treaty countries. Canada has bilateral tax agreements with a number of countries around the world. The purpose of these treaties is to reduce or eliminate the incidence of double taxation. The country to which you are emigrating will obviously have its own tax system, even if it is not based exclusively on an income tax regime.

International Withholding Tax Rates[15]

Country	Alimony	Dividends	Periodic Pension Payments	Periodic Annuity Payments	Lump Sum	Pension Annuity Interest	Trust Income	Estate/ Royalties	Rent Immovable
Argentine Republic	0	10/15	15	15	25	12.5	25	3/5/10/15	25
Australia	25	15	15	15/25	15/25	15	15	10	25
Austria	0	15	25	25	25	15	15	10	25
Bangladesh	0	15	15	15/25	25	15	25	10	25
Barbados	0	15	15	15/25	25	15	15	10	25
Belgium	0	15	25	25	25	15	15	10	25
Brazil	25	15/25	25	25	25	15	25	15/25	25
Cameroon	25	15/20	25	25	25	15/20	0	15/20	25
China	25	10/15	25	25	25	10	25	10	25
Cyprus	0	15	15	15/25	25	15	15	10	25
Czech & Slovak Federal Republic	0	10/15	15	15	25	10	15	10	25
Denmark	25	15	0	0	0/25	15	25	15	15
Dominican Republic	0	18	18	18/25	25	18	18	18	25
Egypt	25	15/20	25	25	25	15	15	15	25
Estonia	0	5/15	15	10	25	10	15	10	25
Finland	25	10/15	20	15	25	10	15	10	15
France	0	10/15	25	25	25	10	15	10	25
Germany	0	15	25	25	25	15	25	10	25
Guyana	0	15	25	25	25	15/25	25	10	25
Hungary	0	5/10/15	15	10/25	25	10	15	10	25
India	25	15/25	25	25	25	15	25	25	25
Indonesia	0	15	15	15/25	25	15	25	15	25

International Withholding Tax Rates continued

Country	Alimony	Dividends	Periodic Pension Payments	Periodic Annuity Payments	Lump Sum	Pension Annuity Interest	Trust Income	Estate/ Royalties	Rent Immovable
Ireland	15	15	0	0	15	15	15	15	15
Israel	0	15	15	15/25	25	15	15	15	25
Italy	25	15	15	25	25	15	25	10	25
Ivory Coast	25	15/18	15	15	25	15	25	10	25
Jamaica	0	15/22.5	25	15/15	25	15	15	10	25
Japan	25	10/15	25	25	25	10	25	10	25
Kazakhstan	0	10/15	15	15	25	10	0	10	25
Kenya	25	15/25	15	15/25	25	15	25	15	25
Korea	25	15	25	25	25	15	25	15	25
Latvia	0	5/15	15	10	25	10	15	10	25
Liberia	0	15	25	20/25	25	20/15	20	10/15/20	25
Lithuania	0	15	0/25	20	25	15/20	0	10/15/20	25
Luxembourg	0	5/10/15	25	25	25	15	15	10	25
Malaysia	25	15	15	15/25	25	15	15	15	25
Malta	0	15	15	15/25	25	15	15	10	25
Mexico	0	10/15	15	15	25	15	15	15	25
Morocco	25	15	25	25	25	15	25	5/10	25
Netherlands	0	10/15	15	15	25	10	15	10	25
New Zealand	25	15	15	15/25	15/25	15	15	15	25
Nigeria	25	12.5/15	25	25	25	12.5	25	12.5	25
Norway	0	15	0	0	25	15	15	15	25
Pakistan	15	15/20	25	25	25	15/25	15	15/20	25
Papua New Guinea	25	15/25	15	15/25	25	10	25	10	25

International Withholding Tax Rates continued

Country	Alimony	Dividends	Periodic Pension Payments	Periodic Annuity Payments	Lump Sum	Pension Annuity Interest	Trust Income	Estate/ Royalties	Rent Immovable
Philippines	25	15/25	25	25	25	15	25	10	25
Poland	0	15	15	15/25	25	15	15	10	25
Romania	25	15	15	25	25	15	15	15	25
Russian Federation		10/15				10		10	25
Singapore	15	15	25	25	25	15	15	15	25
South Africa		5/15				10	25	6/10	25
Spain	0	15	15	15/25	25	15	25	10	25
Sri Lanka	0	15	15	15/25	25	15	15	10	25
Sweden	0	15	25	25	25	15	15	10	25
Switzerland	0	15	15	15/25	25	15	25	10	25
Tanzania		20/25	15	15	0	15		20	
Thailand	25	15/20	25	25	25	15	15	5/15	25
Trinidad & Tobago	25	5/15	15	15	0/25	10	25	10	25
Tunisia	25	15	25	25	25	15	15	5/20	25
Ukraine		5/25	25	25	25	10	15	10	25
United Kingdom	0	10/15	0	10/25	25	10	15	10	25
United States	0	6/15	15	15/25	25	15	15	10	25
USSR	25	15	25	25	25	15	25	10	25
Zambia	25	15	15	15/25	25	15	15	15	25
Zimbabwe	0	10/15/20	15	15	25	15	15	10	25

Consequently, during your emigration process, you will most likely still be responsible for tax on income generated in Canada, while simultaneously being responsible for tax in your new jurisdiction. What tax treaties enable you to do is avoid having to pay tax twice by allowing you to exempt income in one country or claim a tax credit in your new jurisdiction equal to the tax paid in Canada.

The table shown above, "International Withholding Tax Rates," is by no means complete and is included for illustrative purposes only. If you are considering non-residency, you should enlist the help of an accountant who specializes in the area of international and non-residency taxation.

The Ties That Bind

Unlike the U.S. model, the Canadian income tax system is based on residency, not citizenship; therefore by becoming a non-resident and cutting your ties with Canada, you can in essence completely distance yourself from all taxes associated with living in Canada. Sounds easy enough, but there is more here than meets the eye. Becoming a non-resident is a process that requires diligent planning in order to meet some very specific and not-so-specific requirements. In fact, the term *residence* is divided into two separate definitions for Revenue Canada's purposes: *factual* residence and *deemed* residence. The most obvious factors in determining factual residence are the location of your primary residence, family ties (i.e., spouse and/or children) and your employment/economic situation. The factors in determining deemed residence are applied to individuals who are normally resident elsewhere yet remain in Canada for more than 183 days of a given calendar year or individuals who are normally resident Canadians but who have been posted outside Canada (e.g., military personnel and civil servants).

In order to become non-resident, you must demonstrate that your non-residency status is in fact permanent. Leaving Canada to accept a two-year contract in a foreign jurisdiction with the intent of returning after said contract is completed will most likely be challenged, since it will be presumed you were a deemed resident for that period unless you can demonstrate that you did sever all residential ties with Canada. If, however, you are leaving Canada to work or retire for more than two years and you do successfully sever all necessary ties, you can be considered a bona fide non-resident for tax purposes.

I have already mentioned that different types of ties with Canada must be severed as part of demonstrating that you really intend to become non-resident. These fall into two categories, primary ties and secondary ties. As a rule, if you are leaving Canada to become a true non-resident, sell the house. This is clearly the primary tie that links you to Canada. Renting your home to a relative or friend is not considered arm's-length and could easily end up ensuring that you become a deemed resident by virtue of the fact that you did not actually dispose of your property. If your spouse and dependents remain in Canada during your absence, you will also be considered a resident of Canada unless you are legally separated and have severed all other residential ties with Canada. If you are a single person, this is obviously not a consideration unless you are supporting a resident Canadian in a dwelling maintained or occupied by you in Canada and, after your departure, you continue to support that person in that dwelling. In this case, Revenue Canada considers you to have retained a significant residential tie and may treat you as a resident of Canada for tax purposes.

After the primary considerations have been addressed, there are secondary issues an individual must contend with, primarily the disposition of other property and social ties such as:

- Vacation properties
- Automobiles, boats, planes, etc.
- Bank accounts, credit cards, securities accounts, etc.
- Canadian driver's licence
- Provincial medical coverage
- Memberships including churches, synagogues, recreational and social clubs, professional organizations[16]

This list is by no means exhaustive and should be viewed as a preliminary guide since the factors that will determine an individual's status are unique to that individual. However, the devil is always in the details, and this is usually the area where people fail to plan diligently or alternatively adopt a cavalier attitude with regard to what they actually retain in Canada. When I was becoming a non-resident, I heard the story of a man who had become non-resident and over five years later was determined to be deemed a resident by Revenue Canada simply because of the ties he had maintained. His business travel regularly brought him back home so for simplicity and cost-effectiveness he began staying at his parents' house, in his childhood room, whenever he returned. Over the years, his visits became more and more frequent. For convenience, he also started to maintain a modest wardrobe at his parents' house and even went so far as to buy a second-hand car to save money on car rentals. In the end, it was determined that he had a significant presence and was responsible for taxes owing on the time spent in Canada. Defeating your non-residency status for the sake of convenience is not very wise considering all the effort it takes to become non-resident in the first place. Remember: Big Brother is watching.

To add to the fun and games, the Canadian government recently introduced a departure tax system for people who emigrated from Canada after October 1, 1996. The rules impose a deemed disposition of all worldwide assets of the emigrating Canadian at fair market value, with exception given to Canadian real estate and certain Canadian-based business assets and pensions. Moreover, tax must be paid on all accrued capital gains on worldwide assets at the time of emigration, including the shares of private Canadian companies. In the past, it was possible to emigrate without having to pay tax on such shares until the emigrant could possibly qualify for treaty protection in the new jurisdiction. This measure reflects a tightening of the emigration rules for Canadians and is part of the general anti-avoidance campaign being waged by Ottawa. Departure reporting was not mandatory in the past, but the government's view of perceived abuses has clearly moved it in this punitive direction. Needless to say, these rules also have stiff penalties for failure to disclose at time of emigration.

The Big Questions

The non-residency option is ultimately dependent on many issues specific to each potential jurisdiction: climate, lifestyle, range of activities, cost of living, cost of housing and, of course, degree of tax-efficiency or tax advantages from which to conduct your financial affairs. A simple exercise is to start by listing all of the characteristics of your ideal jurisdiction, then list the amenities that you cannot do without (e.g., if you have children, the education system and schools and healthcare facilities).

Cost of living is a major issue, particularly if you are looking for sunnier climes since many Caribbean jurisdictions are U.S.-dollar-based; on top of that, most have import duties on all goods brought in. So while Cheerios may be $3.75 at your local supermarket back home, in Nassau, for example, they'll be approximately US$6. I remember the first time I went grocery shopping with my wife shortly after we arrived in the Bahamas. I nearly fainted. "Six bucks U.S. for Cheerios!" My wife calmly took the box from my hand and placed it in the cart and said, "It's true that, back in Canada, Cheerios are about $4 a box, but you had to make over $8 in order to net the $4 to buy them. So in actual fact, our purchasing power is almost at par, and the exchange rate is really not a factor since we live and work in a U.S.-dollar-based, but tax-free economy." Of course, she was right. After about six months of acclimatizing my sensibilities to the local economy, sticker shock was no longer a factor. What was a shock was shopping back in Canada in a declining Canadian dollar environment.

Culture is another important factor, and a highly personal one at that. The Caribbean offers many jurisdictions that are very close to North America and easily accessible for Canadians who want to explore opportunities for residency: friendly, familiar, foreign and near, etc. Many European countries offer the same basic benefits as their Caribbean counterparts; for the more adventurous or those with European ties, there can be tremendous benefits. Accessing continental Europe and its many cities and cultures is easier and less expensive than trying to do so from the other side of the pond. Remember, it's the 90s: you do not have to be domiciled in the same location as your assets or even your business. However, I've found through discussions with existing non-residents, many of them older, that distance and time differences are inhibiting factors. Choose the location that best meets your needs on an asset management or business level, then the location for living that best suits you.

Regardless of your choice, it is important to research as many locations as possible in order to get a feel for what various jurisdictions have to offer beyond tax-efficiency or bilateral tax agreements. Start by browsing in the travel section of your local bookstore; find the country-specific or region-specific publications that interest and start to answer some of your primary questions. Many international and/or offshore financial publications such as *Offshore Finance Canada*, *Offshore Investment*, *Offshore Outlook* and *Shore to Shore* profile multiple jurisdictions in their issues. If you have specific questions or are in need of additional information, these publications are an excellent resource. If you have an advisor already working on your behalf, ask for any additional information they may have, or, better yet, introductions to their international contacts.

Becoming a non-resident and master of your own financial house in a low or no-tax jurisdiction is a dream many people have and even more are beginning to realize. Even a straightforward move to the United States can yield financial benefits via the numerous deductions and allowances still available in their tax system. The investment and business opportunities that exist globally are immeasurable and the potential for reward is great. But what can't be overlooked in this process are the adjustments to life and lifestyle that may be necessary to realize your dream. Healthcare, housing, insurance, amenities, food, clothing, transportation, social activities, education—all these factors that are part of everyday life are going to change. Consequently, you'll need to examine them carefully to ensure that you and your family's happiness and stability can thrive in a new jurisdiction. Something as simple as going to the corner store for milk or the local video store for a movie rental can take on a whole new meaning in a different country. Be prepared because the initial cultural shock can be disconcerting.

CHAPTER 6

to trust or not TO TRUST

If you mention the word "offshore" in conversation, invariably the subject of trusts will be raised. In this chapter, I will attempt to introduce the basic trust concepts and some of the many variables involved in establishing, administering and settling trusts. I will also explore the duties and obligations of trustees and some of the legal pitfalls and caveats associated with trusts. Be forewarned that this is a complex, even dry, area of estate and financial planning, associated as it is with concepts that date back far into the mists of time.

Trust structures have been in existence for hundreds of years and can range from the straightforward to the almost surreal. One of the more amusing trusts of which I was recently made aware was established exclusively for women offspring of the English Rothman family of tobacco fame in the 19th century. Only female members of the family were eligible to be beneficiaries until one Aunt Bessie or Aunt Gertie or whatever decided to try her luck at breaking the bank at Monte Carlo. She failed—to the impoverishment of the rest of her female kinsmen in perpetuity.

In general, trusts are essentially understood to be a fiduciary relationship between the person who is relinquishing control of some or all of his or her assets to a trusted advisor (the trustee) for the benefit of a defined person(s), group or organization (the beneficiary). Trusts are recognized in common law jurisdictions but not in many civil law jurisdictions and Asian countries. What is unfortunate, however, is that trusts are now marketed to individuals like so many other financial products to avoid taxes.

The fact that a trust is not a product but in reality a strictly defined legal relationship has been lost somewhere along the way. The trust relationship was originally developed as a means of ensuring the avoidance of feudal dues and has therefore been concerned with the mitigation of taxes from the beginning. There are, however, many other and better reasons for using trusts. Of all of the reasons for establishing a trust, the ability to avoid complex probate proceedings in the case of a sizable or multinational estate is the most valuable.

Offshore trusts appeal to individuals from many different backgrounds and with differing needs, but most are looking for two things above all else: certainty and confidentiality, both while they are alive and after their death. Anyone who wishes to preserve or protect substantial financial assets while optimizing the return on those assets in seeking to pass them on to their families and future generations is a candidate for a trust. As mentioned, trust structures can range from the simple to the most complex, but estate planning rather than tax-efficiency should be the primary motivation behind establishing an offshore trust.

Typical trust clients also come from all over the world. Europeans, particularly those from civil law jurisdictions, are concerned not only with protecting their assets but also with passing assets on after their death to their intended beneficiaries, rather than having their beneficiaries determined by their governments under forced heirship laws.

U.S. citizens, who live in what is arguably the world's most litigious society, want to protect their wealth from unforeseen future circumstances which could leave them, and their families, financially ruined. Canadians are increasingly concerned about a gloomy domestic economic situation, with foreign exchange controls and wealth taxes being viewed as a real possibility. Many Canadians also own property in Florida or other states and often neglect the fact that upon their death they may be liable for U.S. estate taxes. Latin Americans wish to protect their entrepreneurial wealth from any future political or economic uncertainty. Asians are used to living with great uncertainty, and particularly after the Asian meltdown of 1997–98, the attractiveness of trust structures for asset protection and security shines bright. As you can see, the demand for offshore trust structures reflects a veritable United Nations of people and needs.

In establishing an offshore trust, your trustee will require information from you to ensure that the assets you wish to place in trust are unencumbered (that is, they are not criminally related and have no current or contingent liabilities against them). This is usually possible with the aid of an accountant's statement and a letter from your lawyer or bankers. The majority of trustees will also put a limit on the amount you may transfer into the trust to a maximum of 60% of your total net worth. Most trustees will also structure the trust so that it is as tax-efficient as possible. The trustee should therefore be familiar with the tax laws of your home country, as well as with the laws of the jurisdiction in which your trust will be domiciled.

Once the trust has been established, you will need to decide where the assets will be physically held (or custodied), and who will manage the investment of the trust assets. If you wish to have greater involvement in the day-to-day management of the trust's assets, an underlying company may also be established, and you or your representative can be appointed as an officer of the company. Assets may be custodied at a bank of your choice, although a large international offshore bank is typically recommended. It is also important to determine the amount of reporting you wish to receive from the custodial bank beyond monthly statements.

The time involved in establishing an offshore trust varies according to how much tax advice must be sought from the client's own jurisdiction. Provided that the client has all the necessary information prepared, a trust can be established within one week. Many trust companies have inhouse lawyers to help in the drafting of the trust documentation. However, each client must also get competent professional advice from his or her own country.

The cost of establishing an offshore trust varies from trustee to trustee and will depend on how much legal work is required. There are also annual fees based on a percentage of the assets held in the trust with a minimum annual fee. A general rule is that total assets in trust should amount to at least $500,000 for a trust to be a viable option.

An Indispensable Tool in Financial and Estate Planning

As cannot be stressed too often, an offshore trust is a legal agreement between three different parties to ensure the long-term benefit of capital by children, grandchildren and other beneficiaries as determined by the original owner of that capital. Here's how it works.

In an offshore trust, personal assets are transferred by an individual investor to a third-party trustee, who holds and administers those assets on behalf of the beneficiaries named by the creator of the trust. As a result, the creator (settlor) of the trust ensures that his or her designated beneficiaries will receive the income and capital growth accruing from the assets held in trust, while removing those assets from direct taxation, inheritance duties or any threat of seizure or confiscation, and enjoying complete confidentiality and freedom of investment as guaranteed by the laws of the jurisdiction in which the trust is domiciled. The trustee ensures that the settlor's wishes are respected and that trust assets are managed in the best interests of the beneficiaries. However, the trustee can be changed at the discretion of the settlor at any time. The beneficiaries, having been designated by the settlor, may receive income and/or capital from the trust's assets during and after the lifetime of the settlor. The settlor can change the designated beneficiaries at any time, and historically has also been able to be designated as a beneficiary of an offshore trust in his or her own right, although this has been subject to abuse and is changing.

Typically, wealthy individuals like to decide for themselves how, where and to whom their assets will be passed on their death. Given its historical role as a financial and estate planning tool, the trust vehicle is probably the ideal vehicle to achieve this. While a will can achieve some of these objectives, a trust effectively transfers ownership of assets to professional trustees who have been provided with defined objectives by the settlor as to how the assets are to be held and administered and for whose benefit. Death always involves changes in family structure and ownership or passing on of assets. Wills, while effective in the simplest terms, are not effective or even efficient methods of passing on assets. With a will, it is necessary to obtain probate on death. Probate is a public process that is usually fraught with delays and expense. If a wealthy individual has left several wills in several jurisdictions identifying several assets, it will then be necessary to obtain probate for each and every will outstanding. A properly prepared trust can avoid the bureaucracy, expense and delays, which so often occur following death.[17]

Setting up a trust to be an efficient vehicle that allows for the enjoyment of the income from assets during the course of one's lifetime and subsequently passes on the enjoyment of those same assets to designated beneficiaries must be properly drafted and executed in order to be upheld. Recent court decisions in the area of trust administration, particularly where settlors retained control of the trust through their own lifetimes, have resulted in the trusts being set aside as invalid, therefore negating the desired result of passing on assets efficiently.

In the past, trusts were an efficient way of mitigating income, capital gains and inheritance taxes, but as recent legislative initiatives in Canada contained in bill C-92 and similar initiatives in the United States and United Kingdom have demonstrated, the ability to avoid taxes through the use of trusts has become severely restricted for persons domiciled in these jurisdictions. These legislative initiatives provide for the imposition of steep penalties for failure to declare trust assets, income from trusts and acknowledgment of the formation of trusts.[18]

When planning an offshore trust for the benefit of Canadian resident taxpayers for whatever reason, you must consider Canadian income tax considerations. The rules under the *Favourable* and the new rules introduced in 1997 are as complex as they are voluminous. Once again, there are obvious and not-so-obvious rules designed to trip up the neophyte and the misinformed. Transfer of taxable Canadian property (real estate, equities, bonds, private shares of a corporation, etc.) to a trust by a Canadian resident settlor will in essence be considered a deemed disposition and be subject to tax on income and capital gains. Interestingly, where the settlor is considered the sole beneficial owner of the trust, it could be reasonably argued that these tax implications would not apply since the transfer would be to the settlor him/herself. But while this sounds like a loophole, it is not. Under the attribution rules, the right of reversion states that if the settlor is a beneficiary of the trust or the trust allows the trust property to revert to that person, he or she may be taxable on the income or capital gains of the trust. In order for the settlor to be free of any potential taxation, the trust must be irrevocable and the settlor must not be a beneficiary or retain any powers or control over the trust. Under these same rules are the provisions for non-arm's length transactions between the settlor, beneficiaries and persons related to the beneficiaries. In essence, loans from related parties to each other as a means of establishing a trust or reducing income can be attributed back to the person who loaned the property if any income or capital gain is realized. Non-resident trusts are subject to the same level of taxation on income and capital gains generated in Canada as non-resident individuals unless they are located in a treaty jurisdiction that provides for reduction or elimination of the 25% Canadian withholding tax. The FAPI rules also come into play in trust matters relating to beneficiaries, the trust property and other possible related properties.

Non-resident trusts can provide the possibility of deferring or possibly avoiding Canadian tax implications when non-Canadian property is held by a non-resident trust and the income therefrom is accumulated in the trust if the rules are followed diligently and understood properly. The rules associated with trusts and non-resident trusts, as repeated, are numerous and complex; they must be carefully reviewed in conjunction with the involvement of a Canadian tax expert long before any action is taken in order to avoid any unexpected surprises.

In the past, when tax revenue was raised primarily on the sale of goods and services, the need for establishing trusts in offshore jurisdictions was slight. But through this century, as governments moved toward direct taxation of income and investments, the need for and uses of offshore jurisdictions and their associated tools, such as trusts and corporate structures, began their rise to prominence. Many jurisdictions have begun the move back toward indirect forms of taxation such as lowering the rate of income tax and raising the rate of sales and value-added taxes, making the use of offshore jurisdictions less relevant. It has yet to dawn on Canada's politicians that a move in this direction would result in a lessening of the flight of capital from Canada's high rates of direct taxation and release a great deal of the capital that is currently locked up in trust in Canada's financial institutions, through fear of the tax on capital gains, to freely re-enter the Canadian economy. The requirements and associated penalties contained within Bill C-92 are possibly having the opposite effect of what this legislation was designed to achieve, since many Canadians venturing offshore are now doing so almost entirely out of a sense of anger and with the attitude that assets placed offshore will never be declared or even repatriated into the Canadian economy. My suggestion to Ottawa would be to stop wasting taxpayers' time and money in drafting draconian legislation that in effect will have the opposite effect of what it intended to accomplish. The freeing of capital in Canada will have the desired result of increasing government revenues and stabilizing the Canadian economy from within.

Trusts have always been concerned with the protection of assets, but what has developed over the past few years has been the development of the asset protection or creditor protection trust (see below). This type of trust has been driven mainly as a result of the enormous awards of damages handed down by U.S. courts in civil cases, and this type of trust has been directed mainly to U.S. citizens. Canadians have had limited exposure to this type of trust but interest has been on the rise of late. A word or two of caution is in order concerning asset protection trusts (APTs). Increasingly, this type of trust is being set aside in courts to determine whether the trust was established to truly protect against potential creditors or established to defraud existing creditors or the claims of creditors that could reasonably have been anticipated. More importantly, some jurisdictions which are promoting asset protection-type trusts are receiving widespread criticism since their legislation in many instances allows the settlor to retain control over the trust assets, and as such, if contested in court may not be considered a trust at all.[19]

Professionals such as doctors, lawyers and business owners are increasingly looking to trusts as a form of additional liability insurance where they can place a portion of their assets and thereby protect them from frivolous lawsuits or malpractice suits. While this has become, in essence, a side-effect of trust law and the many modified trust laws that exists in offshore jurisdictions, caution should be exercised when considering this avenue since the trust may very well end up becoming part of the suit if it is not properly executed.

It would probably be wise for the individual considering a trust to use a jurisdiction with sound trust law and a straightforward trust structure as opposed to one that promotes its asset protection advantages, since such a choice, if challenged, would raise the question whether the trust was established to defeat creditors as its primary motivation.

It has been a generally accepted rule that the wealth created by a self-made entrepreneur will be dissipated by the third generation ("Shirtsleeves to shirtsleeves in three generations"). A trust can no doubt preserve family assets or even operating businesses by transferring these assets to professional trustees and therefore not allowing future generations to squander them. Entire businesses can be preserved for generations by transferring the controlling interest to the professional trustees and imposing restrictions on the sale of shares by those trustees for future generations. The trust, however, must be properly drafted and set up to ensure that the assets have passed into the ownership and control of the trustees. If this is not done properly and control is retained by the settlor or member of the first generation, the trust can be set aside as a sham by members of the second or even third generation.

Whom Do You Trust?

The choice of jurisdiction in which you establish an offshore trust is not a consideration to be made lightly. Your choice of jurisdiction should be decided on the type of trust you are considering or the type of assets to be placed in the trust. Factors such as tax environment, trust law, judicial system, political stability, professional services and communications all have to be part of the decision-making process. This is a kind of checklist of what to look for in making your decision about establishing an offshore trust.

Tax Environment

While jurisdictions such as Canada, the United Kingdom and the United States have excellent trust law, they are not very favourable tax environments in which to establish a trust. New Zealand, on the other hand, has excellent trust law, and provides tax exemptions for the trust and trustee if the settlor is not a New Zealand resident and the trust does not have New Zealand–source income. There will also be no New Zealand tax liability for beneficiaries provided they too are not New Zealand residents. A foreign trust with New Zealand trustees has no reporting requirements in New Zealand and can make use of New Zealand's network of tax treaties for the beneficiaries. A working relationship with a representative of the Canadian legal community who specializes in this area is a good starting point for most people, since they can help you determine the jurisdiction best for you.

Trust Legislation

A jurisdiction whose trust legislation is based on English equity law is the most sensible place to start. Offshore jurisdictions that have introduced their own trust laws or modified their existing trust laws to be more user-friendly must be thoroughly reviewed. As mentioned in the asset protection section, many of the offshore jurisdictions that have introduced asset or creditor protection legislation may be in conflict with the fundamental law of trusts when it comes to the ownership and control of trust assets and, if contested, may be set aside as some legal relationship other than a trust. Remember that a trust is a legal relationship existing between the trustee and the beneficiaries which is recognized by and enforceable under the law of equity. For example, trusts formed in the jurisdictions of Guernsey and Jersey, whose trust laws are not equity-based, will be regarded as trusts in any legal proceedings brought forth in those jurisdictions, but they may be viewed as a different legal relationship in the courts of another jurisdiction. While this has not been an issue for Guernsey and Jersey due to their excellent reputations, the increasing pressure being placed on trusts in other offshore jurisdictions will most probably result in a redefinition of their trust and associated laws.

Judicial System

In the area of trusts, it is sometimes necessary for the trustee to seek direction through the courts, and from time to time disputes can arise between trustees and beneficiaries as well as tax authorities. For these reasons it is imperative that the jurisdiction you choose have a good judiciary, i.e., judges who understand the sometimes complicated legal matters associated with trusts. Older jurisdictions such as Isle of Man, Bermuda, Guernsey and Jersey have very good judiciaries, and in fact much modern trust case law has been developed in these jurisdictions.

Political and Economic Stability

Not much needs to be said here. Since protecting assets and investments is the primary focus of establishing a trust, the stability of any given jurisdiction should be high on your priority list. The Bahamas, for example, has over 300 years of uninterrupted democratic government, and its proximity to North America ensures a sizable influx of U.S. dollars through tourism, adding to the economic stability of the country.

Professional Services

It takes many years for a jurisdiction to establish itself as an mature offshore financial and trust centre. The existence of requisite legal, accounting and banking services is paramount to the establishment and subsequent success of any jurisdiction. On top of these services, there needs to exist a real supervisory or regulatory system that monitors the activities of the practitioners of a given jurisdiction and can provide guidance to both practitioners and individuals. Again, this you will find only in established offshore jurisdictions.

Communications and Infrastructure

It is stating the obvious, but it is also essential: when a trust exists in an offshore jurisdiction, there needs to be a good communications infrastructure in place or headaches will surely follow. The settlor and subsequently the beneficiaries who are domiciled elsewhere must be able to communicate efficiently with the trustees, and the trustees need to be able to communicate efficiently with third parties around the world. Ease of transportation to and from the jurisdiction should also be a consideration, since it may be necessary to visit the jurisdiction occasionally (but never in the winter, when it might be too warm). It is also helpful that modern airports, telex, fax, Internet access and so on exist.

Caveat Emptor

Thirty years ago, it was a common enough occurrence for a baby boomer's father to move assets into an offshore trust structure in a recognized jurisdiction with the intention of preserving them for family and heirs. The reasons were concerns about estate taxes, fears regarding domestic political and economic instability, growing restrictions on foreign investment, etc. As the people who established these arrangements thirty years ago die, the validity and effectiveness of these trusts are coming under attack from disappointed heirs and relatives, former spouses, tax authorities and creditors. As I mentioned before, trusts have recently been set aside in a number of legal cases for a number of reasons:

- The settlor retained control of the trust assets through his or her lifetime, therefore rendering the trust a sham
- The assets of the trust were situated in a jurisdiction that does not recognize trusts
- The trust did not conform with the essential criteria of equity law
- The trust was poorly drafted and prepared, rendering it void for uncertainty
- Even properly drafted and prepared trusts have come under attack for the way they were administered by the trustees.

In creating an offshore trust structure, proper execution is everything. Be warned.

Ramifications of Some Important Legal Decisions

Because trust law is "living" law, a function of particular legal decisions as well as actual legislation, attention must be paid to the state of legal precedents in understanding what can and cannot be done with trusts. Some recent litigation and resulting decisions are illuminating.

In *Rahman v. Chase Bank Trust Company (CI) Ltd. and Others* (1991) JLR 103, the leading case when discussing trust litigation, a Mrs. Rahman was successful in having the trust established by her late husband determined to be a sham. In the view of the court, Mr. Rahman never intended to lose control of the assets in the trust and made all decisions as to the management and investment of those assets, only notifying the trustees periodically. This case was and is an object lesson on what professional advisors and trustees should not do. A trust essentially provides that the settlor relinquish 100% control of the assets to the trustees. In the United States, the courts are addressing the issue of effective control by applying the "alter ego" theory to trusts as well as to asset holding companies. Very few people are willing to give up absolute control of their assets to professional trustees to manage and administer.[20, 21] What developed out of this reluctance to cede control to trustees were forms of direction given to the trustees by the settlor. The letter of wishes has been the most common method for the settlor to express a form of direction over the administration of trust assets. The letter of wishes must be a non-binding, confidential document that merely expresses the wishes of the settlor without binding the trustees to execute those wishes if they feel they should use their discretion in some other manner. The letter of wishes should also be prepared after the trust has been established so that the letter could not be considered part of the trust itself. The reason the letter should be expressed as confidential is that the contents are not to be disclosed to the beneficiaries or a third party in the normal course of affairs. An even better form is to have the trustees record the settlor's wishes as a file note. This is an informal and confidential way for the settlor to express his or her wishes and minimize the likelihood that the note could be considered part of the trust.

Some people have gone even further by appointing a protector. The protector is normally a family advisor such as a lawyer, accountant or family member. The role of the protector is to ensure that the wishes of the settlor are being met but not a means of exercising control by the settlor. The protector's powers should not extend to making decisions on the part of the trustees and thereby negating their discretionary role. The protector is there to ensure that the best interests of the beneficiaries are being met. The duties of the protector are dependent on the terms of his or her appointment and generally extend to the best interests of the beneficiaries and reviewing the trustee's performance. If a protector is given powers to direct the trustees regarding the distribution of income or capital, this could void the trust since the protector could be considered an agent of the settlor.[22]

Letters of wishes and the appointment of protectors are not as common as they were in the recent past, and the potential problems associated with having them are seen as good reasons to avoid them. Individuals should select a reliable professional trustee instead of trying to retain control of trust assets through a letter of wishes or protector, which in the long run could become a liability.

The consequences for trustees of trusts that are held to be invalid, shams or alter egos are growing in seriousness. Under these circumstances, the trustee is considered nothing more than a nominee for the settlor who remains in de facto control of the assets. Any inconsistency with regard to the trustee's actions in the area of control can also be considered unlawful. The trustees will have to repay fees plus interest as well as make good on any losses caused by distributions to beneficiaries other than the settlor or, if deceased, his or her estate. More and more, trustees are being held accountable in many cases involving trusts.

Another area of concern for trustees is the possibility of being held in breach of trust for failure to invest the assets of the trust in a manner consistent with the settlor's wishes or even modern portfolio theory. Many offshore institutions with which trust assets have been placed invariably invested the money with only one aim in mind: capital preservation. As a result, many beneficiaries are in the process of discovering or will soon discover that their family's offshore trust portfolio consists of CDs, Treasury bills and call accounts (cash and cash equivalents). All very safe and proper—and all totally underperforming a diversified portfolio of stocks, bonds and cash. In other words, much of the capital appreciation experienced by the offshore trust would have accrued from capital contributions and not the result of asset growth. This would be equivalent to securing your retirement future exclusively on the basis of your annual RRSP contributions, rather than through the compounding effect of the investment growth of those contributions over time. No wonder many beneficiaries and even settlors themselves have begun asking some very pointed questions about the relative meagerness of their financial portfolios. Why? Far too often, offshore investment has been marketed on the basis of privacy, confidentiality, asset protection, estate planning and tax-efficiency—which are all well and good, but investment performance was not typically part of the equation.

I was approached by a beneficiary of a sizable trust who was quite upset over the fact that the assets his father had been placing in an offshore trust for over thirty years had returns that only averaged approximately 5.25% annually. On closer examination, it became apparent that the trust company had viewed these assets strictly in a one-dimensional manner. Privacy and security were the primary concerns. Investment returns were at best a secondary consideration. Interestingly enough, the father in question was a successful investor at home, fully understanding the value of a balanced portfolio, but why this did not extend to his offshore asset management strategy was no mystery. Too many investors have viewed offshore investment as a "cloak and dagger" affair, thereby dismissing all of the basic tenets of personal financial and investment planning. It should be noted that privacy and confidentiality are inherent in any offshore trust. What tended to happen in the past was that the trustee would invest in lower-risk or even no-risk investments, believing this form of so-called prudence would be rewarded with a problem-free transition to the beneficiaries. Unfortunately for many trustees, they did not consider that the beneficiaries whom they were "protecting" would be as well educated and knowledgeable in the areas of personal finance and investments as many of the baby boom generation.

In two other cases in the recent past where the investment management of trust assets was called into question, the trustees involved were brought to court: one unsuccessfully, the other successfully. The learned judge in *Nestlé v. National Westminster Bank Plc* (20/6/88 unreported) observed: "Modern trustees acting within their investment powers are entitled to be judged by the standards of current portfolio theory, which emphasizes the risk level of the entire portfolio rather than the risk attaching to each investment taken in isolation."[23]

In *Nestlé*, the plaintiff contended that the funds she became entitled to on the death of her father in 1986 and which totalled £269,203 should have been in excess of £1 million considering that the trust had been established in 1922. The bank was held to have misunderstood the investment clause in the will that established the trust. It also failed in its duty to review the investments regularly and failed to take legal advice as to the scope of its powers under the will. Unfortunately for the plaintiff, the burden was on her to prove that she had suffered loss as a result of the bank's breaches of duty. In the view of the judge and subsequently in the court of appeal, she failed to do so.

In *Nestlé*, the potential liability for trustees became glaringly apparent, but they were successful in resisting a claim for restitution because the plaintiff was unable to prove loss. However, in the recent case *Mulligan, Hampton and Others v. PGG Trust Limited and Others* (1996) High Court of New Zealand CP 772/92, the trustees were not so lucky. Breach of trust was alleged, the allegation being that the trustees took no steps to counter the effects of inflation over the life of the trust and that the real value of the trust capital had been eroded. The trust in question was a will trust that came into effect on the death of the testator Mr. Mulligan in 1949. The widow, Bessie Mulligan, received a legacy and a life interest, which did not stop until her death in 1990 at the age of 90. At that point, the capital became divisible between the ten nieces and nephews of the testator. In 1965, when the major asset of the Mulligan estate (a farm) was sold, the trust fund was worth NZ$108,000. According to expert evidence on behalf of the plaintiffs (the nephews and nieces), the equivalent inflation-adjusted figure by 1990 would have been NZ$1,368,000.

The first defendant, PGG Trust Limited, and Mrs. Mulligan had been a co-trustee of the trust fund. Throughout the 25 years from 1965 to 1990, the trust was invested in fixed-interest investments and as a result Bessie Mulligan enjoyed a good level of income. On her death, she had an estate of NZ$686,000, which she left to relatives on her side of the family. In contrast, the trust fund was worth only NZ$102,000, an amount that could not purchase a residential home in 1990; in 1965, the trust fund could have purchased 14 such properties.

One of the main issues in the case against the trustees was lack of even-handedness in that the interests of the life tenant were preferred to those of the beneficiaries. The evidence showed that although PGG Trust Limited, a professional trustee, was well aware of the need to diversify, it had not done so because Bessie Mulligan had opposed any change in investment policy. The judge held that PGG Trust Limited had failed in its duty as trustee because it should have insisted on advising its co-trustee of the need to diversify. In taking the easy way out and avoiding a conflict with Bessie Mulligan, it had failed in the performance of its duties as a professional trustee and thereby denied Mrs. Mulligan the advice and assistance which she deserved. It was also held that Mrs. Mulligan had been guilty of breach of trust in failing to fulfill her duty of trusteeship to the beneficiaries. The judge concluded that, by the 1970s, prudent trustees would have invested 40% of the trust fund in equities, and the failure to do so had resulted in a loss of $170,640. Both trustees were at fault and therefore jointly liable. In the case of Mrs. Mulligan, the liability to make restitution fell on her estate.

The Mulligan case was not simply a matter of a professional trustee being guilty of breach of trust for failure to diversify investments. There were two trustees, one lay and the other professional, and it was to a large extent because the lay trustee was uncooperative that prudent investment decisions were not made. However, the case does show that where, for whatever reason, trustees allow a fund to be reduced in value through failure to manage portfolio risk properly, they can be sued for breach of trust and will be ordered to make good any loss that can be proved.[24]

There are other types of trust which have been the subject of legal action and would be considered invalid, such as the international beneficiary or World Wildlife Federation trusts. This trust structure is typically set up by a dummy settlor who gives a nominal amount of money to the trustee, and the trust deed names the World Wildlife Federation, Red Cross or some other charitable organization as discretionary beneficiary with the power to name further beneficiaries at a later date. Typically, no other beneficiaries are formally appointed, even through a letter of wishes indicating the true settlor's preferences. The trustee, usually an International Business Company (IBC) owned by an investment advisor, will provide funds to the true settlor on an as-needed basis. Very few records are kept except for statements and valuations. Of course, the charitable organization is not informed that it is a beneficiary nor is there really any intention of benefiting the organization. The fundamental problem with this type of arrangement is the failure to identify beneficiaries. The charitable organization's appointment is false, and no other beneficiaries have been identified; under these circumstances, the trust, if challenged, may be held void for uncertainty. Moreover, if the charitable organization becomes aware that it is a named beneficiary, through the public records of the legal system, it may end up sitting behind the settlor in court, smiling. This has already happened in a number of cases.

How to Select a Trustee

Choosing the right trustee will depend on the circumstances and nature of your trust. Take the time to choose a trustee in whom you have absolute confidence whether it be a corporate or individual trustee. For a small trust that has been set up to provide for a family member, there is much merit in considering another family member or a trusted family advisor to oversee the trust. For larger trusts with multiple beneficiaries and possibly multiple jurisdictions, it would be wise to consider the choice of a bank or institutional trustee. Typically, this type is backed by larger institutions with a wide range of services and larger financial resources if any problems should arise. Much consideration must also be given to the back office or administrative capabilities of the trustee and their organization, since trusts are sometimes involved in large and complicated transactions requiring swift and efficient execution. Another consideration when choosing a corporate trustee is cost; but in the offshore world, the adage "You get what you pay for" does not always hold true. Costs can vary, sometimes greatly, depending on the needs and requirements of the trust. Ask your advisor for introductions to more than one trustee in order to compare the size, scope, range of services available and, of course, costs before making a decision. Typically, costs will be based on the value of the assets involved or a fixed charge when the trust is established. Thereafter, the trust will be charged a fixed annual fee, and any additional work on the trust will be charged on a time basis. Some corporate trustees will quote a fixed annual fee with no additional charges for time once the nature of the trust and its administrative considerations have been taken into account.

Are Offshore Trusts Worth It After All?

The uses and varieties of offshore trusts are complicated and merit the full attention of any individual who wants or needs to establish one. Consideration must be given to every detail, such as choice of advisor(s), choice of jurisdiction, choice of trustee and choice of investments. Off-the-shelf-type trust arrangements that promise absolute control should be avoided as pointed out above. As the wealth of individuals increases, their need to establish a sense of control over their assets also increases, and moving assets from their jurisdiction offshore for protection, business and estate planning purposes are considerations worth making. Canada, the United States and other large jurisdictions have enacted legislative measures to try and put an end to this activity. Like the little boy with his finger in the dike trying to hold back the water, this is a futile gesture, as the flow of funds continues and new instruments are created, seemingly overnight, in an effort to deal effectively with these legislative prohibitions. While these same governments have been commendably successful in stemming the tide of money laundering and extreme forms of tax evasion, trying to control the financial affairs and future of their people in this way is dangerous politics.

Summary—All About Offshore Trusts

- Confidentiality and anonymity of ownership of financial assets
- Continuance of existing management of a family business and effective distribution of assets to chosen heirs with avoidance of testamentary problems
- Tax and financial and estate planning convenience
- Protection from foreign exchange controls
- Protection from public sequestration
- Protection against personal lawsuits
- Protection of assets against the breakup of a relationship, including marriage
- Possible deferral and/or reduction of personal income taxes, capital gains tax and wealth and/or death duties for settlor

CHAPTER 7

the ABCs of IBCs and OTHER CORPORATE STRUCTURES

You may have caught the 1950s period flick entitled *A Touch of Mink*, in which Cary Grant seems to be flying down to Bermuda every other day with or without Doris Day. There's more than a little verisimilitude to this particular romantic comedy. The choice of Bermuda may have been accidental, but it is apposite since Bermuda was the birthplace of the offshore company, now commonly termed the IBC, and a destination of choice for the globetrotting businessman of the 1950s and 1960s.

An IBC (International Business Company) or offshore company is a unique structure originally designed to facilitate international commerce. While IBCs still have an important commercial role, they have more often than not ended up serving as holding companies for individual investors' real or financial assets, portfolios and related investment management activity. As our focus is offshore investing, we'll consider IBCs largely in that light.

By definition, an IBC is a legal entity incorporated in an offshore jurisdiction for commercial or personal purposes. While the IBC itself is a relative newcomer to the world of offshore (see below), it has its antecedents in the *exempt company* concept developed by Bermuda during the 1940s and 50s. Bermuda was really among the first of the offshore jurisdictions to discover that "renting the reef" could produce significant domestic benefits. At the same time, U.S. and international corporations were stuck with relatively high rates of corporate tax on their global revenues; in addition, tax rates varied considerably depending on the requirements of each of the countries in which they were operating. Bermuda, not a tax haven but a tax-free jurisdiction, proposed a simple solution: by permitting corporations to consolidate their international revenues in one centre, they could in the process legitimately avoid the separate tax burdens imposed by other countries. The international business company was born.

This little bit of history is important, because it illustrates how IBCs and associated corporate structures have grown from their commercial roots. Now employed in most Caribbean jurisdictions, IBCs have superseded any other form of corporate or business structure. It is also interesting to note how IBCs have become pillars of the local economies. In Bermuda, for example, international business accounts for about 25% of total GDP.

The development of the modern IBC dates back to 1984, when the government of the British Virgin Islands (BVI) enacted the *International Companies Act.* This brilliant piece of legislation recognized the fact that individuals and companies were in need of less regulation in conducting their business affairs internationally. Needless to say, the new act was an instant success, ensuring as it did ease of incorporation, flexibility, minimal disclosure requirements and no BVI taxation on the establishment of an IBC.

Since 1984, various jurisdictions such as Antigua, the Bahamas, Belize, the Cayman Islands and the Turks & Caicos have either amended their corporate laws or copied those of the BVI in order to capitalize on the obvious popularity of IBCs. A large part of that popularity stems from the fact that an IBC is an efficient and economical entity, which typically can be set up for just US$1,000–$2,000. Fees vary considerably by jurisdiction and the perceived value of each jurisdiction: exempt companies domiciled in Bermuda charge for cachet; the beachfront IBC offered in the 19

Turks & Caicos will cost considerably less.

Since the basic principle behind an IBC is to separate the taxable individual or entity from the source of that legal "person's" source of income, an IBC in essence represents the same basic form of incorporation as exists in Canada but with some outstanding additional benefits. Most importantly, IBC legislation in Caribbean jurisdictions has been specifically designed to attract foreign businesses and business people by permitting the creation of corporate structures that can be incorporated quickly and managed under simplified legal and administrative procedures.

How an IBC Works

An IBC is a third man instrument: there's you, your assets and the third-party IBC which controls those assets. In this sense, an IBC is really analogous to a trust structure. Instead of owning assets directly, an individual owns shares in his or her IBC, which in turn legally controls the investor's assets. Once removed from owning assets directly, an individual is no longer liable for tax on income or capital gains accruing from those assets (depending on the choice and style of those invested assets), and complete investor confidentiality is assured. These are the hallmarks of IBCs offered by most offshore jurisdictions today.

Since incorporating an IBC involves a change in ownership of assets, those assets have to come from someplace. In the case of a commercial IBC, which holds the ownership of an active business, the assets are essentially retained earnings derived from the cash flow generated by annual sales activity. In the case of personal IBCs, assets tend to be real property or financial, typically an investment portfolio. As IBCs offer complete flexibility for both companies and individuals, they are also often used to own large assets such as houses, vacation properties or yachts.

Once an investor has incorporated an IBC, he or she retains ultimate control over the IBC through its board of directors, which manages the underlying assets of the company. Alternatively, IBC ownership may be placed in an offshore trust. The board of directors need not be an elaborate affair. Typically, one or two nominee directors (usually local accountants or lawyers) will suffice; the IBC investor may or may not be a director depending on preference. There is no requirement as to the number of shareholders and an IBC may be wholly owned by one person or entity.

The requirements governing the composition of boards of directors vary by jurisdiction. There are benefits to shopping around. In the

Bahamas, for example, there is no need for nominee directors. Another major attraction of Bahamian IBCs is that there is no requirement to file public notices of officers, directors or shareholders and there is no need to publish financial statements. Shareholders, directors and officers can also reside anywhere in the world. A unique aspect of Bahamian IBCs not to be overlooked is the fact that a corporate entity itself can act as a shareholder, director or officer. This is extremely useful if you conduct business in multiple jurisdictions and wish to maintain your confidentiality. The uses of an IBC can be as flexible as the needs of the company or individual who establishes them. In addition, an IBC can provide an extra layer of protection and confidentiality along with estate planning flexibility for investors or company owners.

As we have seen, the concept behind an IBC is simple and incorporating an IBC is relatively easy. IBCs have no minimum authorized or issued capital requirement, which may be denominated in any currency. In the Bahamas, the standard Memorandum of Association fixes the authorized share capital at US$5,000, as this is the maximum authorized capital permitted for the minimum annual licence fee payment. Share capital is by no means fixed and can be adjusted to meet the needs of the individual(s) or corporate entity forming the IBC. This adjustment in share capital is usually associated with more complex business structures and would incur additional costs. Generally, IBCs are exempt from income and similar taxes; stamp duty on documents; foreign exchange control regulations; and death duties on the estates of deceased shareholders. IBCs pay registration fees on incorporation and an annual licence fee based on the IBC's authorized capital over their lifetime. IBC registration normally takes only 48 hours and the red tape is minimal.

The basic reason IBCs afford a high degree of confidentiality is that only limited filing requirements must be met. Only the name of the company, its registered agent's name and address, and the company's Memorandum and Articles of Association, including any amendments, must be filed with the registrar. Again, the names and addresses of the company's directors and shareholders are not filed in the Bahamas, providing the investor with total privacy.

The Advantages of Establishing an IBC

The main advantages of an IBC are confidentiality, asset protection, tax-efficient asset management and financial/estate planning flexibility. All of an investor's worldwide assets may be controlled by an IBC, with the beneficial ownership of the shares of the company remaining strictly confidential. The investor retains ultimate control over the composition of the IBC's board of directors, which in turn manages the underlying assets. Advantages of particular jurisdictions also come into play. For example, in the Bahamas these include its secrecy laws, taxfree status and reputation as a leading international offshore financial centre with access to a wide range of full-service trust, banking and brokerage firms.

IBCs offer complete flexibility for companies and individuals. For individual investors, IBCs are often used to manage investment portfolios or own large assets such as a house or yacht. Assets held in this fashion are exempt from income, capital gains and inheritance taxes within the jurisdiction of incorporation. Companies involved in international trade or privately owned businesses can benefit from tax-efficiency and continuity of ownership through an IBC structure. For instance, IBCs are useful for reinvoicing, transfer pricing and other international corporate cash management functions. International sports and rock stars also use the IBC structure to manage the tax-efficiency of their global earnings. For professionals, IBCs may be used for billing purposes under the terms of an employment contract with positive tax consequences, and an offshore company can acquire the exclusive rights to professional services performed by the IBC's beneficial owner.

Asset protection is a topic that generates a great deal of interest among business owners large and small, and another draw of the IBC structure. If McDonald's can be successfully sued for serving hot coffee, is your business safe? In the "sue me, sue you" society in which we live, many investors and business owners are concerned with protecting themselves, their families and their accumulated wealth from unexpected lawsuits and judgments. Canada is slowly becoming as litigious a society as the United States.

Still others are concerned about political and economic instability in Canada and the results this may have on their economic future. Combining an IBC with an effective asset protection structure effectively renders assets immune from seizure, lawsuits, divorce settlements or other actions arising from court judgments.

Another key benefit of IBCs is portfolio diversification. Moving non-lifestyle assets to an offshore jurisdiction is an effective way to diversify your holdings globally. The privacy and protection inherent in an IBC can also be augmented if an IBC is combined with a suitable trust vehicle. The shares of the IBC can be held in an asset protection trust, thereby effectively transferring ownership of the company to the trust. The asset protection trust is a vehicle unto itself, which can provide an additional layer of privacy and confidentiality. However, offshore trusts are becoming more and more a hard sell in common law jurisdictions as trusts in general have come under increased pressure and litigation from both Revenue Canada authorities trying to close loopholes and trust beneficiaries themselves concerned about asset underperformance and its direct impact on their trust incomes.

The beauty of an IBC is that by definition it can do anything a human being can do with regard to commerce and investing. As a shell, it exists to serve as a holding company for assets. Bank accounts and investment portfolios are only the tip of the iceberg. Two years ago, a long-time client asked what I knew about art and more precisely the great Impressionists. He knew of an upcoming auction of some rare watercolors and wanted to know if his IBC could act in the auction. Of course his company could, but his directors and officers would have to act on behalf of the company. So we attended the auction and successfully bid on three items, which now hang in his vacation home as part of his extensive collection. By the way, the house is owned by his IBC as well. If planned and properly structured, IBCs provide complete flexibility and highly effective asset protection; some also rank as among the finest private museums in the world.

Know the Company You Keep

The principal restriction that applies to most IBCs is that they may not own real estate in the jurisdiction in which they were incorporated or engage in business activity in that jurisdiction. IBC are also restricted from providing the registered office for other companies or conducting insurance, reinsurance, banking or trust functions. In other words, a Bahamian IBC cannot own a hotel in the Bahamas, but it may own a Cayman business and vice versa. However, IBCs can engage the professional services of lawyers and accountants, lease office space and open accounts with banks, trust and investment management companies or brokers in their jurisdiction of incorporation. Outside its home jurisdiction, an IBC may undertake any activity in the ordinary course of business providing that it is prescribed in its Articles of Association.

IBCs are typically exempt from income tax, capital gains or transaction taxes in their home jurisdiction for a period of 20–30 years (as always, depending on the jurisdiction) from date of incorporation. This should not be viewed as a drawback, since you can always move your IBC to another jurisdiction and hence prolong its life.

IBCs do not provide any immediate Canadian tax benefits per se, but under the Foreign Accrual Property Income (FAPI) rules of the Canadian *Income Tax Act* (ITA), active business income earned and retained in a foreign jurisdiction need not, in certain cases, be reported or be subject to Canadian income tax. Therefore, an IBC that directly carries on active business or makes qualified investments considered active under the FAPI rules may benefit from this exemption. Active refers to the day-to-day operation of a viable business in the respective foreign jurisdiction.

Many investors make the naive assumption that, by opening an IBC and subsequently transferring assets through the IBC to a bank or brokerage account, they are free from reporting the income and capital gains accruing from these assets and are consequently exempt from taxation. Nothing could be further from the truth. An IBC is simply an incorporated shell or vehicle; it is what the IBC is invested in or through that counts. I have approached this topic in Chapter 5.

Given this basic explanation of the IBC structure, it should be clear that before calling up the Off-the-Shelf Offshore Company Formation Inc.'s advertisements prominently displayed in offshore periodicals to "buy" an IBC, you should give some serious thought as to what exactly it is you want to achieve. It is especially critical to enlist the help of seriously competent advisors *at home* before venturing offshore. The advisor you spoke to on your last visit to the Bahamas, Cayman, BVI, Turks & Caicos, Nevis, etc. is probably more than competent in the areas of company formation and relevant legislation, but may not be familiar with the amount of information needed to deal effectively with and provide solutions for a resident Canadian taxpayer. Canada has an extensive and highly professional legal community specializing in offshore; this is a much sounder initial step than structuring an IBC solely on the basis of the information and advice of a competent but non-Canadian advisor.

It is also worth remembering that not all offshore jurisdictions are sandy beaches and swaying palm trees. In financial terms, offshore means anywhere that is not onshore. Onshore means the jurisdiction from which you want to escape/remove assets/leave your spouse, etc. Therefore, someone from Monaco or France would consider the United States as offshore for tax planning purposes, while a Canadian would not. In addition, choice of jurisdiction must follow utility or function. For example, Ireland or the United Kingdom (including dependents such as Barbados) can be a better choice of jurisdiction for the Canadian RRSP holder who wants to become non-resident than, say, the Turks & Caicos or the Bahamas (neither of which offers tax breaks on the collapse and subsequent transfer of RRSP assets, because both lack a tax treaty with Canada). Therefore, your offshore planner/advisor needs to know a great deal about different jurisdictions and their inherent advantages and disadvantages as they pertain to what you want to accomplish with your IBC.

The Active Versus Passive Test

A friend of mine who fancies himself an investment guru once scoured the offshore world to find investments and/or funds that meet the criteria under the FAPI rules (see above). He reported to me quite triumphantly that he had found no fewer than 850 funds that dealt effectively with FAPI. I smiled and then inquired if these investments also met the criteria as set out under section 94.1 of the *Income Tax Act*, also known as the offshore investment fund rules. Section 94.1 clearly states that holding stocks, bonds, commodities and real estate in an offshore account (including IBCs) for investment/income purposes is considered "passive" portfolio investment, and consequently permissible, but subject to an annual deemed income tax based on the original book value of the invested assets. In other words, if an investor purchased $150,000 worth of equities through an offshore entity and, come tax time, declared this investment (as indeed he or she should), he or she would be subject to deemed income on that investment regardless of its current market value and dividend status. Section 94.1 has probably been the greatest deterrent to Canadian investors looking offshore.

There are, however, exemptions under 94.1. Investments in actively managed commodity and/or derivative pools and certain hybrid investments can qualify. My friend insisted that commodities and derivatives were not for him, so I said, "What about hybrids?" Most investors have never heard of hybrids despite the fact that they are probably already invested in hybrid funds. For example, RRSP-eligible global equity and bond funds are the domestic equivalent of an offshore hybrid fund. How does a fund that to all appearances is 100% foreign content qualify as 100% RRSP eligible? There are several ways of achieving this. For example, the fund manager can make use of index or fixed-income futures, currency derivatives and swaps (swaps, in simple terms, are the transference of performance from one underlying portfolio to another) in combination with Canadian Treasury bills to tip the scale in terms of being deemed a Canadian investment.

Hybrids offshore, like those onshore, can achieve two functions: provide access to investments that would otherwise be unacceptable under the Canadian rules and confer the potential for deferring taxes. In the case of my friend, his offshore portfolio, which is held through an IBC, now comprises both investments that are exempted under 94.1 and ones that are non-exempted. In other words, some are considered active and others passive. Hence, under FAPI the IBC is required to report and be subject to Canadian taxes only on those investments that are non-exempted. This individual has mitigated his tax situation by making use of exempted investments and is effectively deferring taxes on those investments until such time as he sells and/or repatriates the gains and/or assets to Canada. In addition to the tax deferral advantage, these investments were also beneficial because they were both unique and not available in Canada, i.e., they provided enhanced portfolio diversification. Since so much cloak-and-dagger stuff has been written about offshore and taxes, it is sometimes salutary to reflect that the legitimate deferral of taxes can be as useful as out-and-out tax avoidance. You get an equivalent benefit and not go to jail. In essence, an offshore investment portfolio can be likened to having the world's largest RRSP with absolutely no contribution limits.

IBCs Mean Business

Many small to medium-sized Canadian businesses are starting to recognize the value of establishing a presence offshore. One example that comes to mind is an import/export company I have worked with that specializes in importing rare fabrics into Canada. The principals spend a great deal of time and effort in the Middle East and Asia locating suppliers and sources of product, subsequently negotiating the purchase price (in U.S. dollars) for these goods to be shipped to Canada.

When I first met the owners, they were happy with the success and profitability of their business. Their only real concern was their ability to compete by paying U.S. dollars for product derived from conducting business in Canada—in other words, how to maintain their profit margins. Since they purchased all of their fabrics abroad, they were hostages to the relative weakness of the Canadian dollar; any drop would reduce their margins by adversely affecting their already competitive pricing. The cost of getting to and from the sources of their products would also be greater, not to mention the expense of shipping the goods back. They also expressed concerns that they had no financial management expertise or knowledge of currency management and hedging but would still like a solution.

I introduced them to a lawyer I know who specializes in international trade and business management. His comment: "Classic trading company. Do you want to locate in a low-tax or no-tax jurisdiction?" The clients looked at each other, looked at me and then looked across the table at the lawyer and said, "What do you mean no-tax?" The lawyer then proceeded to tell them that under the circumstances it would be advisable to establish a company in a tax-efficient jurisdiction. This company would act as agent for the Canadian company by purchasing and subsequently shipping goods to Canada. The beauty of this arrangement was that the offshore agent would purchase the goods at their traditional wholesale prices in U.S. dollars and then sell the goods to the Canadian company at a higher value (i.e., the international company buys goods at US$100 and sells the same goods to the Canadian company at US$105). The U.S. dollar profit arising from the difference would be accumulated in either a low-tax or a no-tax jurisdiction.

By trapping the U.S. dollar difference in an offshore jurisdiction and mitigating taxes (legally) on that profit, the importers were in a much better position to manage their margins. This is a viable option for many businesses in Canada. The only real drawback is the greed factor—for example, buying goods internationally for $100 and in turn selling them to an affiliated Canadian company for $200 instead of a more reasonable $105. The other drawback is the fact that many people become so enamoured of the IBC form that they overlook the structure needed to make an offshore trading company work effectively. With such trading companies, it is important to choose an offshore jurisdiction that has good communications, as shipping and documentation can be critical to the overall plan. So, for example, an offshore trading company administered out of Hong Kong would be highly suitable for the above example. If trade is occurring within the European Union necessitating VAT registration, the Isle of Man would be the recommended venue. If trade were occurring in Latin America, the Cayman Islands or Bahamas would be suitable. And so on. There is no cookie-cutter solution here, as every company's circumstances are unique, but these principles apply to most commercial IBC formations worldwide.

Bahamian Limited Partnerships

The origin of limited partnerships (LPs) lies in European law. They have seen very little use offshore until recently. However, an array of offshore jurisdictions have been introducing the LP structure lately. The benefits of limited partnerships are no secret to U.S. and Canadian taxpayers. They have been used for many years for everything from funding oil and gas exploration plays to paying the deferred load on mutual fund sales and other applications of a similar nature. Most important, they have provided favourable tax benefits as well as a safeguard against liability for debts.

The essence of the limited partnership is that it has two classes of member: limited partners, who are discouraged from taking any part in management but whose liability is limited entirely to their contribution paid into the partnership; and the general partner or partners, who have unlimited liability, but have the entire management responsibility. The LP itself does not have a legal "personality," and is therefore treated as a partnership for tax purposes. Where there is a large number of members, a trustee is required to hold the LP's assets.

Under the Bahamian *Exempted Limited Partnerships Act, 1995*, the advantages of using the LP structure have been enhanced by allowing access to the facilities of the tax-free offshore centre and provision for complete asset protection against creditors—good news for people whose professional, business or private lives make them vulnerable to lawsuits. Under the Act, there must be at least one general partner to manage the partnership assets and one limited partner.

The general partner must be a person resident in the Bahamas, a company incorporated or registered in the Bahamas or another partnership. The general partner is liable for all debts and obligations of the partnership, and legal proceedings can only be instituted by or against the general partner. Limited partners need not be Bahamian residents nor, in the case of companies, incorporated or registered there. Active management of the partnership by limited partners is discouraged, as they may be held liable by third parties for debts if the partnership becomes insolvent. A number of activities provided for under the Act are not regarded as "active management." For example, limited partners can be officers or directors of a corporate general partner, or provide advisory services to a general partner without running afoul of the provisions of the legislation. However, they must avoid creating the impression that the limited partner and the general partner are one and the same.

In the Bahamas, an IBC usually acts as general partner, conferring the advantage of limited liability. The individual or any entity controlled by the individual is then named as limited partner and can also become an officer of the IBC acting as general partner to maintain some control over the partnership. If trouble appears on the horizon, the officer can resign his or her position and cut all ties with the IBC to limit any potential personal liability.

Exempted limited partnerships must keep a registered office in the Bahamas, with the general partner maintaining a register of the address, amount and date of any payment representing a return of any part of the contribution of any partner. The general partner is also obliged to maintain a register of partnership interests that have been mortgaged.[25]

Advantages of the LP Structure

There are many advantages to LPs. Asset protection is a prime example. A creditor who obtains a court judgment against one of the limited partners cannot seize assets held in the name of the partnership. Nor can he or she demand the partnership be wound up and the debtor's share of the assets paid to him or her. The creditor can only hope to claim payments made to the limited partner on an incidental basis, but as the general partner tends to have discretion over whether to make such payments, there is often little to seize.

Additional asset protection advantages occur when liquid assets such as cash or stocks and bonds are transferred from the jurisdiction of U.S. courts to the Bahamian partnership. The holder of an existing U.S. judgment against one of the partners would then have to sue in the Bahamian courts to enforce the judgment. Such creditors face an uphill battle for three reasons. First, the use of an IBC as general or limited partner makes it difficult for creditors to find the limited partnership or its assets. The

IBC is not required to publicly file details of ownership, the identity of officers and directors, nor financial statements of any kind. Limited partnerships with assets held in Bahamian domiciled banks also benefit from the bank secrecy laws of the Bahamas. Second, since the creditor would have to sue in a Bahamian court, he or she would need to engage a Bahamian attorney. Under the rules of the Bahamian Bar Association, Bahamian attorneys are prohibited from practising on a contingency basis, where they are compensated only if they win. In dealing with non-resident clients, Bahamian attorneys invariably seek substantial cash retainers before launching court proceedings. Third, in the case of foreign creditors launching court proceedings in the Bahamas, the defendant will often argue successfully before a Bahamian judge that the creditor, who usually has no real commitment to the Bahamas, should be forced to post a bond for a substantial amount of money in case he or she loses the case and is obliged to pay the defendant's legal expenses.

Exempted limited partnerships, a new device in the range of investment alternatives available to offshore investors, are especially attractive to U.S. taxpayers as properly designed partnerships combining the benefits of favourable tax treatment with the need for asset protection.[26]

There is a vast range of business and company structures available to the offshore planner. Consider the number of countries and territories in the world and the fact that every one of them has business and company forms to offer, some identical to others and others still being a variation on a theme. Then consider the various forms of tax status available. Now take a company formed in one jurisdiction, register that company in a second jurisdiction and make it resident in a third for income tax purposes. You get the idea.

Other Corporate Structures

Like financial products generally, the permutations of the offshore company are literally limited only by the imagination. Here are a few of the best.

Company Limited by Guarantee

These are companies which are essentially mutual. There is no initial capital. Persons can be elected into membership without any cash requirement, although normally each new member is expected to pay an entry subscription upon election to membership at a rate as determined by the directors. However, every member, whether an entry subscription is paid or not, by virtue of election to membership, guarantees to pay a set sum (determined by the Articles of Incorporation) on demand in the event of the company becoming insolvent at liquidation. A member's liability is limited to his guarantee (usually a nominal fee). Thus we have a company with members' liability limited to the extent of this guarantee.

Membership ceases on death or resignation (although, unless specific provision is made, a deceased member's estate may continue to have an equitable interest in the company; this can provide the basis of transferability of members' interests). The subscriptions that have been paid (both the initial entry subscriptions and any subsequent annual subscriptions), are not returnable upon someone ceasing to be a member. In principle, every member has equal voting rights and equal rights to income or capital distributions, should any be made, although flexibility in these matters can be provided to allow for different classes of membership. (e.g., Associate Membership, Non-Voting Membership, etc.) However, it is possible to draft a de facto transferability of membership rights, if required. This is done when such a company is, for example, used as a timeshare resort members' club or country club.[27]

Company Limited by Guarantee and Having Shares

These are companies (sometimes called *hybrid* companies) some of whose members contribute to the capital of the company and acquire rights pro rata to their contribution to the capital (and are issued with shares), but who are additionally required to contribute to capital should the company subsequently go into liquidation while insolvent; and some of whose members are elected into membership without necessarily being required to contribute to the capital on election, but who can be required to contribute to capital should the company subsequently go into liquidation while insolvent. While the non-shareholding members are essentially mutual, the shareholders are not. This gives rise to immense flexibility. In modern terms, we can think of a proprietary club along these lines, which has "owning" members and "customer" members.[28]

Protected Cell Company

This is a new form of company, introduced recently in Guernsey. Everyone will have them shortly. The object of the exercise is to be able to link specific assets to specific share classes, and thereby protect the assets from being included in the general assets of the company. Devised for "Rent a Captive" captive insurance companies, they have great appeal as vehicles for funds. They also have immense attractions for such things as timeshare resorts, in which a specific asset (say an apartment) is to be linked to a specific member.[29]

U.S.-Style Corporations

Only two jurisdictions are significant. Both Panama and Liberia have a form of company modelled on the Delaware Corporation. Neither jurisdiction is as widely used as in former years. The distinguishing feature is the almost complete absence of disclosure requirements.

Limited Liability Company; Limited Life Company; Limited Duration Company; Limited Liability Association; Society with Restricted Liability

This is another group of entities inspired by the U.S. limited liability company. The essence of these vehicles is that they are designed to meet certain criteria under U.S. tax rules. Normally, the objective is that, although they have legal personality, the LLC is treated for U.S. tax purposes as a partnership. I believe that some 48 U.S. states now have this form of entity, pioneered by Wyoming some years ago.

Typically, the limited liability company (LLC) has restricted transferability of shares, with a provision that, upon the "resignation" or wish of a member to transfer/realize his or her shares, the LLC goes into liquidation, or at least reorganization (just as a partnership would). Typically also, the LLC has no directors, with all the members (like partners) participating in management. A manager can be appointed, however, working with delegated powers.

Offshore, the number of jurisdictions permitting this structure is growing. The Caymans, the Bahamas, Turks & Caicos, Nevis, Barbados, Bermuda, Western Samoa, and the Isle of Man all have them with varying quality of legislation.[30]

Anstalt and Stiftung

In Liechtenstein there are two other forms of corporate structure, with strange characteristics. To understand them properly, one needs to be familiar with Roman concepts of fiduciary relationships, and, in particular, the concept of patrimony. In essence, under Roman law, every person has a patrimony of property. The patrimony can be split into two patrimonies, but it cannot be alienated. Thus the idea of the trust is inconceivable, implying as it does that personal patrimony can be owned by somebody else, without the patrimony actually changing.

The Anstalt and the Stiftung are closest to a guarantee company, where the original subscribing member, by whom the capital assets were introduced, remains as the founder, with perpetual and transferable controlling powers. The Anstalt is the form for trading purposes, while the Stiftung is the form for family asset holding purposes. Luxembourg, which is home to tens of thousands of Anstalt, has become one of the premier offshore jurisdictions, partially because of its proximity to the rest of Europe but also because of its innovative regulatory environment.[31]

U.S. and Canadian Tax Treatment of Bahamian Limited Partnerships

If properly designed and implemented, the Bahamian limited partnership can provide considerable asset protection without adverse tax consequences. As noted frequently in this book, the Bahamas has no income tax, capital gains, estate or inheritance tax. However, for the removal of doubt, the Act specifically states that partnerships created under the Act are exempted from such taxes (i.e., in the Bahamas), including business licence fees and stamp duty, for a period of 50 years from the date they are created.

Investment in limited partnerships by U.S. and Canadian taxpayers is "tax-neutral," receiving the same tax treatment as U.S. or Canadian partnerships. Income generated by the partnership flows through to the individual tax returns of the partners. Income of the IBC general partner is treated as dividend income to the owners, as would be the case if the general partner were a U.S. corporation. Although the establishment of the Bahamian IBC and partnership may be taxable under IRC 1491 (US) the taxpayer can elect under IRC 1057 (US) to treat the transfer of assets to the partnership as "a sale or exchange of property for an amount equal in value to the fair market value of the property transferred," thus avoiding excise tax. Transfers of cash to a partnership are not subject to excise tax. Other assets such as stocks or bonds are taxed on their appreciated value, which is the difference between the value of the security on the open market minus its original cost. As the jurisdiction of the U.S. and Canadian courts extends to U.S. and Canadian citizens and individuals and property present in the United States and Canada, cash and securities are the type of assets which should be transferred to the partnership. Real estate in the United States and Canada is obviously less desirable, since it remains subject to U.S. and Canadian courts.

Summary—All About IBCs

- An IBC is a multi-functional, private holding company incorporated offshore.
- All or only some of your worldwide assets may be controlled by your IBC.
- Beneficial ownership of the shares of your IBC remains strictly confidential.
- There is no requirement as to the number of IBC shareholders and an IBC may be wholly owned by one person or entity.
- There is no public record of the directors of an IBC, thereby providing the investor with total privacy.

- The key benefit of an IBC is the assurance of asset protection and investor confidentiality.

- IBCs provide personal financial/estate planning flexibility as well as ease of corporate succession planning.

CHAPTER 8

your offshore TOOLBOX

Talking to individual offshore investors, I have always emphasized that the key benefits associated with offshore investment and business planning are not tax-related. For investors whose financial planning needs have been carefully looked after at home, investment planning offshore can mean the potential for real diversification and a whole new world of investment opportunities. In addition, asset protection in an ever-litigious society, a sound guarantee of the efficient transference of your wealth on death, estate planning flexibility, the ability to expand your business internationally via a friendlier jurisdiction and non-residency are all good reasons to look beyond the crop of anemic solutions to these considerations currently available in Canada.

The questions usually associated with an individual investor's offshore quest are: Whom do I talk to? What type of advisor do I need? What type of institution should I deal with? In turn, the answers to these questions invariably raise more questions.

Offshore financial centres are home to many of the world's largest banks, trust institutions, investment houses and mutual fund companies. They allow you to search the world for opportunities in both emerging and established economies and can provide you with the tools and guidance you need to be successful offshore.

Banking on Offshore

Banking is only part of the solution to effectively invest or protect assets offshore. Several times a week I see Canadian visitors to the islands who, on leaving the cruise ship or disembarking from their flight, make a bee-line for the Nassau branch of the Canadian chartered bank they conduct business with at home. They approach the counter and furtively scan the branch while asking to open an account in a hushed voice. These same individuals are more than surprised when the teller offers resistance. They become equally surprised when they are told that the $5,000, $10,000 or even $20,000 in cash they brought with them will not be accepted. As mentioned previously, cash is no longer an accepted form of deposit by reputable international banks due to the global effort to eliminate the flow of illicit funds. But some further clarification is in order. The Canadian chartered bank branches so obvious throughout the Caribbean (and around the world for that matter) are not there to cater to onshore Canadians. They have been established to serve the banking needs of the citizens and businesses of that locale for savings accounts, chequing accounts, bill payment, loans, credit cards and so on. Furthermore, these branches are discouraged from accepting business from resident Canadians.

In November 1995, there was an article in the *Globe and Mail* that stated the Canadian government would be demanding that the international branches of the Canadian chartered banks begin to disclose information on those accounts belonging to Canadian-resident taxpayers. Obviously, this was met with harsh criticism on the part of the banks and fear on the part of individuals with such accounts. Fortunately, the secrecy provisions of the banking laws of offshore jurisdictions prohibit the disclosure of client information under penalty of law and risk of financial penalties; the possibility of incarceration for bank employees in these jurisdictions was not an option. Many of the Canadian chartered banks instituted changes thereafter, such as altering the Canadian ownership of branches in foreign jurisdictions or not paying interest on the accounts of Canadian residents.

With all of these roadblocks (including not earning any return whatsoever on your money), opening a bank account in an offshore jurisdiction is not a very efficient means of diversification. While your assets may be diversified geographically, interest-bearing accounts in this low- or no-rate environment cannot be considered an effective investment strategy. So where to go from there?

The Allure of Private Banking

Private banking is not new to many Canadians as wealth in Canada has expanded and the chartered banks have introduced newer and better services to accommodate their high-net-worth domestic Canadian clients. Private banking in an offshore environment is a wonderful choice for those individuals looking for a comprehensive financial and investment arrangement—a one-stop shop if you will. Private banking usually consists of standard banking services, investment services such as mutual funds and brokerage, and corporate services for the establishment and management of offshore companies and corporations. Typically, this is handled through a single account with multiple facets or "relationship" account or number. All activities pertaining to the account would be under the watchful eye of your private banker or relationship manager. Many of the large banking institutions that offer private banking services also have a trust operation. This is a convenient solution for many high-net-worth individuals, but not so convenient for someone examining possible offshore options with only a modest portion of his or her assets.

Costs have always been an overriding or even prohibitive factor in offshore investing; in addition, the minimum deposits required by many of the larger financial institutions, private banks and trusts have been substantial. Some will not accept clients with liquid assets of less than $1,000,000; others will accept clients with $150,000, but have an endless series of service charges for just about everything. I once met a prospective client who asked us to provide a proposal in order to win his account. He was already the client of a large institution, but he was not happy with the returns he had earned on his investments and felt that there were better options available. When he received our proposal, he called immediately to ask if we had somehow made an error in our calculation of fees, but I assured him we had not. We eventually won his account and as part of the process reviewed with him his statements from his previous institution. All told, fees associated with managing, administering and investing his assets exceeded 8%. So while his investment returns totalled 12.6% for the year, his net return was only 4.6%. No offshore advantage there.

While it is true that the costs and fees associated with going offshore have historically been greater than in the domestic arena, this sort of thing is unacceptable. Institutions that have not reviewed or are not reviewing their fee structures are in for a big surprise in the very near future as increased global competition for your investment dollar heats up. Many of North America's largest financial institutions are venturing offshore with new products and services that retain the benefits of being offshore with the economies of scale and consequently more reasonable fees associated with domestic investment—a double whammy for the staid offshore industry.

This is not to say that all private banking institutions are not cost-effective. But your choice in a private bank must be balanced against the range of services available (services you will actually use), efficient and cost-effective means of communication for monitoring account activity and generally staying in touch, and a private banking representative with whom you feel comfortable. On that note, one of the main drawbacks with some institutions is staff turnover. Just when you thought you had established a good working relationship with your private banking representative, the next time you call you are informed that your representative has been transferred to another jurisdiction or home. This can cause disruptions and be a source of extreme irritation, since now you have to "break in" your new rep. Ask direct questions pertaining to all of these points and you will find the private banking relationship that best suits your needs.

Independent Advisory or Consulting Firms

Offshore advisors provide comprehensive services ranging from company formation and administration to coordinating banking, investment and trust services either by themselves or through a network of professional relationships; some are generalists, while some only specialize in one area. The choice of advisor should depend on the needs of each individual investor as determined by themselves with the aid of their Canadian advisor. I recommend using a Canadian advisor first, since many advisors in offshore jurisdictions, while they may be generally familiar with some aspects of Canadians and Canadian issues, usually lack either the insight or the recent information needed to make informed decisions. Another option is to find an offshore advisor who is Canadian. As I've mentioned throughout this book, Canadians are everywhere around the world and many offshore and tax-haven jurisdictions have Canadians prominent in their communities.

Comfort is paramount in this relationship, since you cannot make a decision on your choice of advisor entirely on the basis of cost. What you are looking for is an advisor who provides you with the information you need and is prompt and efficient in handling your communications and your affairs; if the comfort level is there as well, this individual is definitely worth the price of admission. Many independent advisory firms also provide access to an established network of professional service providers, such as legal, banking, accounting and trust services. These networking arrangements can be very time-efficient and cost-effective, since the advisor will work on your behalf with these institutions to achieve your plan, as opposed to your having to go out and establish these relationships on your own. Identifying the offshore services you need, not the services that are designed to impress, is also key. While ship registry is an important and impressive service, you want to ensure that your business is not there to defray the overheads of a large offshore institution.

Legal Beagles

Lawyers: either you love 'em or you hate 'em. Offshore, they are as integral a part of the business world as they are at home. In fact, the legal communities of many offshore jurisdictions rival banking in terms of the number of bodies employed. They also provide many of the same services described above and could very well be included in that section. But lawyers are also the people who are most familiar with the legislative initiatives of their own jurisdictions and with the legal and tax issues that confront individuals and businesses from high-tax jurisdictions. I mentioned earlier on that individuals looking offshore for opportunities or relief should first seek the guidance of a representative of the Canadian legal profession who specializes in this area. This is important, because specialist Canadian lawyers will have contacts with many offshore and tax-haven jurisdictions and can provide you with guidance as to the jurisdiction and legal representatives who best meet your needs.

Offshore Mutual Funds—Not to Be Despised

The mutual fund explosion of the past few years has not been solely confined to domestic investment opportunities. Offshore funds have had a concurrent growth pattern over this same period and the investment options available through offshore funds rival those in Canada. Offshore funds, like their onshore counterparts, are managed by a professional investment manager for the benefit of fund investors; the only difference is that they are located (domiciled) in a no-tax or low-tax jurisdiction. Many investors worldwide have experienced the benefits and cost savings associated with mutual fund investing as opposed to assembling a portfolio of individual securities and making the day-to-day investment decisions associated with managing that portfolio. However, offshore funds and fund managers are not faced with the same investment and trading restrictions normally associated with onshore funds; as a result, there are all sorts of very interesting funds available offshore.

Basically, offshore funds have far more freedom than their onshore counterparts. While they are often managed by the same professional managers or institutions with which you are already familiar, they are free from the costly reporting requirements of regulatory bodies and are located in a low- or no-tax jurisdiction. According to the *Micropal Guide to Offshore Investment Funds*, there are now in excess of 5,500 offshore funds currently available, the vast majority being domiciled in Luxembourg and Dublin, Ireland. As to which offshore funds best suit your needs, as always you need to look beyond recent performance. The domicile and the regulatory environment should also be an important part of your decision-making process. For example, before the Bahamas enacted its own mutual fund legislation in 1995, I could very well have started a mutual fund with some fancy marketing material, a fictitious track record and zero capitalization: "Gordon's Offshore Fund; Manager: Gordon; Administrator: Gordon; please make all cheques payable to: Gordon. Next flight leaving Nassau paging passenger: Gordon." So far as other considerations are concerned, all the same rules that apply to domestic fund investments apply offshore.

Discretionary Managed Accounts

Discretionary asset management used to be the domain of the ultra-wealthy. The minimum account size demanded by institutions was typically in the millions of dollars and the associated costs could be elevated as well. Welcome to the 1990s! With the advent of technology and greater global market access, discretionary management is now within reach of the individual investor.

Discretionary management simply means establishing a relationship with a money manager with a defined set of risk/return parameters and an overall investment strategy (as established between the manager and yourself). The money manager is then given discretion to invest your assets in an investment portfolio that best meets those defined characteristics and to rebalance the portfolio when opportunity or market conditions dictate. The real advantage for the investor is access to a money manager or series of managers and investment styles that best meet his or her needs and objectives. In fact, discretionary accounts frequently outperform widely held mutual funds of the same or similar basic investment strategy.

Costs for discretionary accounts have come down over the years but do vary widely from institution to institution. For example, the typical management fee ranges between 0.75 and 1.50% of assets per annum, charged quarterly in arrears. Sounds good compared to the 2 or 3% charged for the typical global fund, but this usually does not include transaction costs (brokerage), custody and banking charges. Depending on the amount of activity in a given account, theses costs can add up. Some institutions, however, now offer discretionary asset management and asset allocation programs (global fund of funds approach) with set fees of between 2 and 2.50% all in. These programs are becoming more and more prevalent as global competition in asset management services heats up. Many of the private banking institutions and independent advisors offshore either have this as part of their range of services or have a corporate relationship that specializes in this area.

The Leap of Faith

Offshore investment and business planning involves a leap of faith for one main reason: distance. The idea that someone will be 1,500, 2,000 or 10,000 miles away from his or her assets is a new and sometimes uncomfortable concept. Never mind that the individual may actually be closer to his or her money than the advisors, since much of the assets can and will be invested via financial centres such as Toronto, Chicago and New York. The idea that money is nothing more than an electronic transmission between financial institutions is a concept some people have a hard time grasping. The first year I worked for an offshore fund company, I got a call from a concerned client during hurricane season who asked, "Is my money safe? I noticed that a hurricane may be heading toward Nassau and I was wondering if you would be taking my money off the island?" After much explanation and hand-holding, I explained that we do not keep clients' money in coconuts tied to a tree nor do we have a treasure chest buried in the sand. His money was invested through our institution and in funds of

Fidelity Investments, Guinness Flight and others. The only real area of concern should be the computer and electronic records of financial institutions that could be at risk during a violent storm, but I assured him that all of our records were backed up electronically and stored in a safe environment. This type of questioning has occurred on more than one occasion and simply illustrates the lack of information or even understanding that people have on the workings of financial institutions on- or offshore.

Finding the Right Advisors

With the dramatic growth of interest in information about offshore financial services, there has been a corresponding increase in the amount of information available through a multitude of channels. The Internet is one that has experienced exponential growth in this area. There are an estimated 3,500 financial Web sites currently available to North American investors, many of which feature offshore financial information.

Caution should be exercised, however, if you, as a Canadian-resident taxpayer, are attempting to conduct your financial affairs over the Net with companies in faraway lands. No matter which medium you receive information from, it should always be scrutinized as to the scope of services being offered. Watch for telltale signs: obvious inaccuracies, possible misrepresentations and clearly dodgy investment schemes. Ask yourself these questions: Are the promises of the service provider pertinent to your particular situation or merely generalized pie-in-the-sky claims? Remember, if it sounds too good to be true, chances are it probably is. Does the offshore service provider have up-to-date information or any knowledge of the Canadian *Income Tax Act* and the rules and regulations that govern Canadian-resident taxpayers? More importantly, do you? Who are the people or companies behind the offshore group? Is the company providing investment management or corporate and trust services, or do they offer a comprehensive suite of services?

These are just some of the basic questions to be asked. All investors, whether onshore or offshore, should arm themselves with as much pertinent information as possible before proceeding with any investment plan.

Equally, they should screen the marketing "fluff" when compiling research material and concentrate on substance, no matter what the source of that material. What I mean by "fluff" would be the equivalent of a would-be consumer researching the purchase of an automobile on the basis of its 0–60 mph performance characteristics alone, with no research or information on fuel-efficiency, handling, safety and warranty features. Sure, we'd all like to have a Ferrari, but a Volvo is far more affordable and much more comfortable when trekking around with the family.

It is also only common sense that the same principles should apply when making financial planning and investment decisions. Avoid the get-rich-quick schemes and concentrate on the "get rich slow" ideas that have been successful for so many for so long. For instance, self-directed RRSPs are a great vehicle for the deferral of taxes for Canadian investors. But they are only as good as the investment decisions made by each investor. The individual who has diligently contributed to a self-directed RRSP on an annual basis and has subsequently built a portfolio of blue chip stocks and provincial and federal bonds, and placed the balance in carefully selected equity mutual funds, will fare far better over the long term than one who sporadically contributes to his or her plan and looks for short-term plays on small-cap resource and technology stocks, always with an eye to making a quick buck. The same applies to offshore financial planning and investment. If you are looking to get rich quick offshore, stay home, buy the Ferrari and tear up the TransCanada. You will have more fun and fewer surprises.

Despite the allure of offshore marketing, a lot of the information you require is much closer than you think. Many of the larger Canadian legal and accounting firms are very well aware of the dos and don'ts of offshore financial planning and investment and can be of great assistance in your research process. Information and insight on issues such as which jurisdictions and advisors are considered to be best equipped to deal with Canadian investors and which structures and investments best meet their overall needs can be just a few local phone calls away.

More on the Net

Many investors are convinced that they are "getting it from the horse's mouth" when they surf the Net and source various international Web sites. The Internet is admittedly a rapidly growing source of high-quality information, featuring many important sites sponsored by large, global financial institutions. Should you take the next step and carry out your financial transactions on the Web? The question of security should be your greatest concern. Security on the Internet is improving, no doubt. You can readily purchase CDs, books, clothing and even big-ticket items like cars, boats and planes online. But do you really want your personal financial affairs to be conducted electronically? The Internet is still largely unregulated when it comes to conducting financial business. As such, it is very much a case of "Buyer beware." The Internet is an efficient means of receiving information, updates and general communications from various financial institutions. The day is coming (very soon) when all of your financial and transactional needs will be accessible with complete security via your PC; but we're not there yet. And while we are clearly living in the McLuhan age of information, where the medium can be as important as the message, it is worth remembering that it is what you do with the information—and not how you access it—that ultimately counts.

CHAPTER 9

BOY, HAVE I GOT A DEAL FOR YOU

The world of offshore finance and investment has not been without its fair share of controversy and glaring headlines. From the Latin American drug cartels and other criminal organizations that used international financial institutions to launder their money in the 1970s and 1980s to the wide-ranging effects of the BCCI scandal just settled recently, there have been any number of highly publicized incidents. Fortunately, the efforts of the world's largest jurisdictions to stem the flow of illicit funds and money laundering activities have been successful to date, and many leading offshore jurisdictions have adopted similar—sometimes even superior—initiatives to protect their legitimate offshore clients and businesses, enhancing their reputations as serious financial centres as a result.

However, it is nearly impossible to regulate everyone most of the time or someone all of the time. Take the case of Nigeria, where the scam discussed under the next heading is estimated to be the third-largest employer in the entire country. Through this scam, individuals have been enticed into parting with a tremendous amount of money through some well-written letters that make the recipients feel as if they were important enough to have been singled out for a substantial windfall. This scam is not an isolated incident occurring only in the offshore world; in fact, the United States Secret Service, Interpol and Royal Canadian Mounted Police have information and examples of this scam on their Web sites. But one thing is certain: if there's a proverbial sucker born every minute onshore, the offshore population must be growing at an exponential rate.

Scams and Scammers—The Nigerian Scam

This is also known as the "advance fee" scam or internationally as the 4-1-9 fraud after the relevant section of the Nigerian penal code that addresses fraud schemes. Nigerian scams are quite creative and constantly changing. I first became aware of this one some years ago when a number of associates began receiving an unsolicited fax from a Dr. So & So who was minister of "God Knows What" in the then Nigerian government and a director of the Nigerian National Petroleum Company (NNPC). The fax asked for assistance in liberating funds that were "overinvoiced" by NNPC and which would be transferred to the account of a foreign individual (you) and not reported to the government if you were to be able to help. The amount of the funds in question was in the tens of millions, usually in the range of US$10–$60 million, and the "commission" payable to the victim for assisting in the liberation of these funds was typically quoted in the 30% range. It was clear that the NNPC must have had the most incredibly incompetent finance department on earth, since it had succeeded in misplacing tens of millions of dollars that are now being made available to you. This was even better than winning the 6/49!

I asked a friend of mine in the legal community what he knew about this, since anyone would consider an unsolicited fax of this nature to be highly irregular. He informed me that the scam had been going on for a long time and that the targets were usually individuals selected fairly randomly, but obviously sharing one thing: a good address. He went on to explain that he knew of a few cases where people had actually followed through and subsequently lost substantial amounts of money. The catch was the advance fee requested in the fax. The fee you were asked to fork over was supposed to cover the administrative costs of setting up your account, completing the necessary paperwork and possibly taking care of bribes to government officials necessary to release the funds (this was only darkly hinted at). The fee typically amounted to tens of thousands of dollars. If you agreed and forwarded the funds, you were graciously thanked by return fax. A short time later, you were contacted again, this time to say that the funds were considerably more than previously estimated, but that there had been complications and would you be so kind as to provide some additional financial assistance? If so, your reward would be that much greater. This, by the way, was the scam within the scam. Obviously, you would never again see one red cent of the money you were to remit the second time, let alone the original commission.

This is only one example of the now dozens of variations of the fax scams emanating from Nigeria. While they have the same mechanics, they have different profiles, the most common of which fall into seven distinct categories:

- Disbursement of funds from wills (You didn't know you had a relative in Nigeria, did you?)
- Contract fraud (COD of goods or services)
- Purchase of real estate
- Conversion of hard currency
- Transfer of funds from overinvoiced contracts other than oil
- Sales of crude oil at below market prices

In nearly all of these cases, there is a real sense of urgency in the way the "investor" communication is packaged: the documents are very official-looking with stamps and pompous seals of state; the confidential nature of the transaction is emphasized again and again; and substantial name-dropping of government ministries and titles is prevalent. This verisimilitude is what entices many individuals into cooperating and forwarding funds to them in the first place. Initially, the intended victim is instructed to provide company letterhead and pro forma invoicing that will be used to show completion of the contract. The reasons for this are to use the victim's letterhead to forge letters of recommendation to entice yet other individuals and to seek travel visas from the American embassy in Lagos, the capital. Once received, the victim is informed that the completed contracts are being approved and the funds will soon be remitted to the individual's personal account. This is when the heat gets turned up. The victim is now confident that the deal will materialize and little stands in the way of success. So when further "complications" arise, he or she willingly forwards even larger sums of money to protect the "investment" and "guarantee" success. Of course, these complications were intended from the beginning and they form the backbone of the scam.

The darker side of these scams surfaces when individuals are requested to travel to Nigeria via a bordering country (this is an important detail, as you will see) to complete the transaction and to be met and thanked by "government officials." Enticed by the amount of money on the table and convinced of the authenticity of the deal in virtue of the official-looking documents and resounding title(s) of the government contact(s), the victim who falls for this trick is the fraudster's masterpiece. When such individuals arrive as they are instructed in a bordering country (to maintain the aura of secrecy surrounding the deal—James Bond never travels direct), they are told that a visa is not necessary to enter Nigeria. The con artists then insinuate the victim into Nigeria through a series of bribes to airport and immigration officials. Unfortunately, it is a serious offense to enter Nigeria without a visa and the fraudsters then use the fact of the individual's illegal entry as a means of extracting additional funds. Threats of violence often accompany this extortion. This had got so out of hand that in June 1995 an American was murdered in Lagos, while pursuing a 4-1-9 scam. Numerous other foreign nationals have been reported missing in Nigeria as well.

We're not talking small change here. It has been estimated that approximately $5 billion worldwide has found its way to Nigeria since 1989 when the scam was first reported. And amazing as it seems, there are several legitimate reasons why the Nigerian advance fee fraud has experienced a dramatic increase in recent years. The Nigerian government blames the problem on mass unemployment, the extended family system, the get-rich-quick syndrome and especially the greed of foreigners. It has also been suspected, and some people have even speculated publicly, that the Nigerian government itself is the scammer. If so, victims have little if any recourse for recovering money lost to 4-1-9 scams. (By the way, the $5 billion figure is only an estimate; it is surmised that a great number of victims do not report their losses out of fear or embarrassment.)

Interpol has reported that the Nigerian scam artists have become so adept and confident in their abilities that they are now contacting previous victims of the basic fax fraud. They pose as Nigerian government officials and internal security service personnel investigating the fraud and attempting to get the victim's money back, again on payment of an up-front fee. And it appears that yet another twist is on the rise. North American "business" people have also been calling individuals stating that they are negotiating very lucrative contracts with Nigeria. All they need is a little up-front money to get the process rolling.

If you receive one of these calls, letters or faxes, do nothing. (A figure illustrating a typical fraud letter is shown in the Appendices.) Don't pay an up-front fee for anything. Do not extend credit for any reason. Never expect assistance from the Nigerian government and don't expect much from the Canadian government on these matters. It is extremely difficult to pursue and prosecute these cases in any really effective manner. There is a 4-1-9 investigation team at RCMP headquarters in Ottawa, but this is not where anyone should direct complaints and inquiries. Regional offices of the RCMP commercial crime division are the best places to forward information, inquiries and data pertaining to this scam. These regional offices provide the central team with all the vital statistics.[32]

Prime Bank Instruments or Roll Programs

While the Nigerian scam complex makes for entertaining reading (unless you've been suckered), this is my personal favourite. The prime bank note or roll programs, as they are commonly referred to, have been around for a long time. The premise behind this scam is that individuals who get involved are actually being asked to join an elite group of sophisticated international investors with access to information and financial instruments normally reserved for only the largest global financial institutions and that by pooling their assets to a substantial amount they can then purchase a "prime bank note." Returns are obviously in the stratosphere and, as such, this exclusive group must maintain its secret and mysterious nature or everyone else would be doing it. It is now estimated that this fraud reaps $10 million a day in the United States alone.

There are hundreds of variations on this easily described fraud. As a case in point, last June I was teamed up on the golf course with three people who had paid good money to attend a conference in the Caribbean on international bank instruments. After I confessed that I'd heard about several of these over the years, none of which worked—and, of course, they never do—one of the members of the trio confided that as Alan Greenspan's (chairman of the U.S. Federal Reserve) sister-in-law was involved, this thing was obviously legit. Presumably the Alan Greenspan of Frostbite Falls, Wisconsin, not Washington, D.C.

The financial principle behind these schemes is always the same. Very impressive-looking documents, supposedly issued by well-known international banks, describe how large global institutions lend each other money by issuing notes with a face value of $100 million or more known as prime bank notes. These same notes are then said to be traded at a discount to par, the differential between their current market value and their value at maturity being the gross margin or profit to the investor, just like Treasury bills and other discount paper. The "profits" often quoted by these schemes have been around 30%, although some have been seen as high as 200%, and the term of the investment can range from 30 days to one or two years. Where the story gains the confidence of the intended victim is a function of the names of the large banks involved, e.g., Barclays, Credit Suisse, etc. There is, of course, no backing for the notes by any of the aforementioned financial institutions. The fraudsters then go on to describe the details of the investment process with sophisticated banking and investment terms that are designed to make the victim feel as if they are not experienced enough in the ways of international high finance to understand; therefore, few questions are asked.

I once attended a small gathering of "select individuals" at the behest of a friend where the secrets of international banking would be revealed. Since I accompanied someone and was therefore not on the invited list, my attendance was initially met with some resistance. But after my friend confided to the presenter, obviously falsely, that I had just sold my company for an amount in the low seven-figure range, I was admitted with open arms and presumably pockets. After signing confidentiality agreements and non-disclosure documents, all of which on closer examination were replete with spelling and grammatical errors, we were ready to be enlightened. The presenter was so well-spoken and had the ability to string together all sorts of exotic financial terms that, had he made sense, he would have put Lou Dobbs out of a job. I looked around the room and, of the seventy-five or so people in attendance, everyone was paying rapt attention. Many of these people were recognizable by name as well as reputation. But not one lawyer, banker or professional investment advisor was in attendance. The presenter laced his description of the investment program with terms such as "prime bank note, irrevocable letter of credit, Federal Reserve guarantee, exclusive and confidential." Then if you weren't convinced by all that, the assembled "consortium" of investors with the guidance of his firm would reap all of these financial rewards in a tax-haven jurisdiction where they would pay no taxes. Some of the attendees began cheering.

During the Q&A, people actually started to describe what they would do with their newfound wealth instead of asking any deeper questions. The ruse was complete. I asked the presenter why, if this process was so private and secretive, he was sharing "our" secret with potentially hundreds more people throughout the week. He looked at me with a puzzled expression and replied, "But I'm not." "Then why do you have this hotel room booked all week"—I had asked the banquet manager—"and what are all those dates and times in the notebook you inadvertently left open on the table?" The presenter handled this with some finesse by confiding that these meetings were with the heads of the financial institutions that would be putting the notes together, which immediately should have raised some alarm bells because not many international bank heads would presumably be having meetings in a suburban Toronto hotel. Seeds of doubt were planted in some attendees, while others who had already counted, banked or spent their imaginary profits glared at me with looks that could kill.

The reasoning behind the group presentation gambit is that since few individuals have the means to participate on their own, the fraudsters describe in great detail how a group of individuals who pool their assets under their guidance can have the same presence as a large international financial institution. All they need is a few of the attendees of these "secret meetings" to bond together with visions of dollar signs dancing in their heads every night for a week or so to reap millions. They also keep the dream alive for a considerable amount of time by advising individuals via telephone, fax or letter that their proceeds are invested and/or reinvested at a better rate than was originally anticipated and that there is a possibility that they can persuade the powers that be to allow additional contributions.

The SEC (Securities and Exchange Commission) in the United States has recently issued warnings on the prevalence of these schemes, as has the International Chamber of Commerce, since it seems that even some professionals have been duped by this scam. The SEC alert stated, "many of the illegal or dubious schemes appear to involve overly complex loan funding. In the eyes of an unsophisticated investor, this complexity may make a questionable investment appear worthwhile. The SEC warns investors and those who may advise them, particularly broker-dealers and investment advisors, of this possible hallmark of fraud and reminds them of a basic rule for avoiding securities fraud: if it looks too good to be true, it probably is."[33]

Beware the RRSP Strip

This is probably the most dangerous scheme to confront Canadian resident taxpayers yet. The scam preys on the fear, anxieties and anger of Canadians for all the reasons and more that have already been cited in this book. The premise here is that Canadian-resident taxpayers can invest the entire proceeds of their self-directed RRSPs in the shares of a private corporate/investment structure designed to create a loss, i.e., structured to go belly-up on purpose. That loss is then declared to the revenue authorities, resulting in a zero RRSP for the investor, since the shares are now worthless. However, in the meantime, the proceeds of the investor's RRSP have found their way to an offshore account (the RRSP has been stripped, geddit?) thanks to the assistance of the domestic advisors who proposed the scheme, less 15–20% commission. Obviously, that's a steep commission run, but it's a lot less than paying tax on a 100% RRSP deregistration. There are a number of variations on the scheme. For example, suppose a Canadian-resident taxpayer who has $500,000 in his or her self-directed RRSP invests in ABC Inc. ABC makes a number of bad investments and/or loans (on paper). One of those loans is to an offshore company and it eats up all the RRSP cash that the shares raised. The offshore company then declares its inability to repay the loan and/or goes bust. The proceeds (i.e., the investor's remaining RRSP capital) have been deposited in an account that has been established for the investor, the 15–20% commission is levied and the investor can now benefit from "tax-free" accumulation and investment, offshore, of the remaining $400,000 or so. Remember, at the same time there is no RRSP left at home to deregister and pay tax on—it's been blown to smithereens by bad investments. This is one simple variation of a scheme gathering steam in Canada.

The reason I say this is so dangerous is that this scheme, while perhaps alluring to the unsophisticated, can be easily challenged by the revenue and finance authorities. If anybody were to suggest it, pause to think before acting foolishly, because:

- Revenue Canada is already well aware of this scheme.
- Even though the assets may have been safely ensconced offshore, this does not preclude investors from their reporting obligations as Canadian resident taxpayers. Remember that you are responsible for reporting all your worldwide income, and the newly introduced rules now have steep penalties for failure to comply.
- Many of the tax experts I have spoken to on this matter, and one source within Revenue Canada itself, consider this scheme to be out-and-out fraud, let alone tax evasion. Since the original investment structure is designed to go belly-up in order to get the funds out of the country, the advisors who promote this scheme have put themselves in a precarious position.
- Finally, I do not expect this to last much longer since, when the authorities finally confront those individuals who have benefited from this scheme and the Canadian advisors who have been promoting it, the penalties and legal repercussions will be felt for a considerable amount of time.

The general point here is that if you are going to live, work, retire and die in Canada, expect to pay taxes. If individuals are concerned about the future of their RRSP assets, they can relocate those assets to a tax-friendly jurisdiction through the annual deregistration of a portion of their RRSP (on which they will pay tax, naturally). Over a period of time, the assets can find their way to a friendlier environment, only the minimum required tax will be paid and, if planned for and invested properly, the investor's assets will benefit from further tax deferral over the life of the investment. While this does not sound as sexy and exciting as the above scheme, it can be effected with relative ease and no risk. Offshore can be likened to having the world's largest self-directed RRSP, with absolutely no contribution limits. True, you have to report your affairs annually, but you are also not limited to the same extent that you are otherwise in Canada. There is a world of investment and tax planning opportunity available to the Canadian investor. It just depends on how you go about it.

Electronic Fraud—Spreading Faster Than a Speeding Mouse

The Nigerian and roll scams are classic examples of successful, long-running frauds. These schemes have been difficult to put an end to and/or prosecute because of their extreme adaptability and the cunning of the fraudsters themselves. This adaptability has made it difficult for regulatory bodies and policing agencies to provide timely information, since these schemes seem to be constantly changing and, of course, the greed factor and naïveté of the general public make them even more difficult to contend with.

What a world we live in!

On that topic, it appears that some people even want to create their own worlds, countries or city states online. While these Web sites do not necessarily have any fraudulent activity associated with them, they and their creators are definitely living in an alternative reality. There are a few sites that profess to be the start of new, independent, kinder, gentler, tax-free countries that will soon be sprouting up in the Caribbean or some other favourable clime under the guidance of a benevolent dictator, spiritual leader or government system that will revolutionize the way society is organized. Some of the "press releases" on these Web sites merit consideration as skits for *This Hour Has 22 Minutes.* Passports to these yet-to-be-established and/or recognized jurisdictions are sometimes available, but did I mention that the majority of their leaders are spouting their rhetoric from the comfort of their suburban U.S. living rooms while they pass laws and assemble potential citizens for their "imaginationstates"?

The Internet is fraught with dubious information sources and scams designed to part you from your hard-earned dollars. While the Net can be a source of tremendous information, caution does need to be exercised. As I have said time and again, the information age is upon us and is changing the way we look at finance, business, life and the world. The Internet was once the domain of government agencies and academics, linked together through a collection of servers located all over the globe. When companies like America Online, Compuserve and Prodigy brought this medium to the public's attention, its commercial possibilities dawned on many businesses and business people, some legit, some not so legit. The earliest forms of commercialization were crude attempts at cyber or electronic commerce (EC is now, I believe, the buzz) such as mass e-mails or spam. The early users reacted negatively to unwanted electronic solicitations. As the Net began to mature, newer and slicker methods of commercialization developed. While the people who have been connected to cyberspace since the pioneer days may already be aware of the pitfalls and schemes now in use, the problem of investment fraud could reach epidemic levels as millions of neophyte surfers join the online cavalcade of what was once the lightly travelled information superhighway.

While the Internet has the potential to educate investors via the multitude of reputable financial Web sites to become better investors, the potential for tragedy exists if cyberspace is eventually regarded as a haven for investment swindlers and securities scams. The financial consumers who could very well be empowered by the wealth of information available on the Internet may end up shunning the medium. Regulators in the United States and Canada are already looking into cases of the manipulation of either little-known equities or "story" stocks. A "story" stock could be a thinly traded issue with an interesting story behind it. The manipulators will pump up the story and post tantalizing messages on multiple commercial bulletin boards to make the issue sound like the greatest get-rich-quick scheme since the dawn of time (or Bre-X). When the stock has gone from pennies to dollars and the promoters have already made their profits and exited, the frequency of their messages on the bulletin boards slows considerably. Such "pump and dump" schemes are starting to become common occurrences. They're hard to stop because online service providers are processing hundreds of thousands of messages daily. Many of the investment-specific messages appearing on commercial bulletin boards are from brokers, investment advisors, newsletters and dealers all promoting their services and products. Though many of these messages offer simple information or advice on stock picking and other investments, there are plenty of direct pitches and open solicitations by what many would term to be unqualified investment advisors.

The combined circulation of the *Globe and Mail, Financial Post* and *Wall Street Journal* falls far short of the reach of someone who posts messages on several of the commercial bulletin board services available. With a few keystrokes, it is possible to reach hundreds of thousands of people with one message. Many of these messages make mention of insider information or announcements pending and encourage a "buy it before the street does" mentality to provide the thrill of exclusivity (once again). The Internet is suffering the same fate that the postal and telephone systems did when they were introduced to the world, when hucksters and swindlers fleeced many unsuspecting users of these newfangled instruments with scams of their own. History is simply repeating itself, only much faster and more efficiently than ever before.

The investor's rules of the road on the information superhighway should be:

- Keep your excitement level and expectations in check. Failure to exercise caution with regard to an unfamiliar investment opportunity can quickly spell trouble. There are no real get-rich-quick methods.

- Don't buy stocks on the basis of online hype. Thinly traded, little-known issues can be moved from pennies to dollars in a few strategic trades by the manipulators with your help. Do your own equity research and don't rely on online information
- Know your source of information. Many Internet bulletin boards allow people to hide their true identities with aliases or "handles." This may easily preclude your being able to ascertain whether the online information is coming from a qualified/registered source or not.
- Recognize all the telltale signs, such as claims of insider information, pending announcements, new products, possible mergers, etc.

The Internet is a wonderful place and its appeal easy to understand. The entire world is at your fingertips. You can chat with someone on the other side of the globe, go shopping for just about anything you can imagine, take a virtual tour of your dream house or look for a new car. And you can afford to buy it all on the basis of the huge profits you expect to reap from trading this little gem of a stock called Yoyodine Virtual Electronics, which according to your investment bulletin board is going to be bigger than Microsoft. Good luck.[34]

CHAPTER 10

offshore investment management

WHERE DO YOU WANT TO GO TODAY?

So far, we have sought to show (1) that privacy, confidentiality, asset protection, and estate, financial and tax planning are all essential hallmarks of the offshore world and (2) how each individual investor's goals can be readily achieved offshore with the right combination of advice and preparation. But offshore means much more than financial planning. In an investment context, offshore is synonymous with global investing. That is because investing offshore is the most efficient way of globally diversifying assets in order to achieve the best possible returns over an extended period of time.

The most important thing to realize, however, is that offshore investing isn't any sort of magical mystery tour. I remember when I first began examining the whole offshore area. At every presentation I attended, I felt as though I was about to be exposed to a new and enigmatic world whose secrets would soon be laid before me; but insight came gradually, like the dance of the seven veils in which the dancer will only remove four veils and no more at any one time. I walked out of many presentations with more questions than I had when I walked in. But offshore is far from being some sort of nebulous Bermuda triangle, and persevering investors will peel back the layers of mythology, misconception and misinformation that have been built up over time to reveal offshore financial, business, investment and estate planning for what they really are.

In fact, offshore investing can be as simple a proposition as holding a portfolio of U.S. securities through an offshore account. On this note, it always amazes me that relatively so few Canadians have enough exposure to the U.S. market, i.e., both stocks and bonds. Long the world's dominant and most mature capital market, the United States offers unparalleled investment breadth and the highest degree of liquidity anywhere. In addition, the U.S. stock market boasts the most comprehensive range of world-class companies in consumer products, finance, communications and technology, global industry leaders whose products and services have the same leading market share internationally as they do at home. On the fixed-income side, the U.S. bond market is the global determinant of interest rates and the safe haven that has displaced gold in any flight to quality. I don't particularly care about current market valuations or interest rate levels, since these are transient—the point is that the United States should be a key component of any serious investor's holdings for the long term. And it's all possible with an offshore portfolio—no foreign content rules, assets denominated in a stable currency, no taxation on interest or capital gains at source, no withholding taxes, no hassles. Offshore, the world is your oyster.

The Case for Offshore Investing

For a long time now, Canadian investors have looked beyond our national borders for diversification, enhanced performance and a hedge against weakness in the value of the Canadian dollar. Each type of international market—developed and emerging, equity and fixed-income—provides unique investment opportunities on its own and at different points in the domestic economic cycle. But as with all investing, the mix of global markets and assets appropriate for each individual will vary according to age, risk tolerance and overall investment objectives.

It's handy to review the key principles behind global investing for Canadian investors and then try to place them in an offshore context. The point is that offshore liberates you from the Canadian market (but it doesn't liberate you from Canadian income tax reporting requirements) and lets you hold the world in your portfolio:

- *Diversification* The limitations of the Canadian stock market, which is still largely resource- and commodity-based, have already been noted. Most importantly, many key industry groups or subgroups are simply not represented in the domestic market and the range of equities available is comparatively meager. In addition, Canada is tiny in terms of overall global market capitalization—less than 3% of the total for equities and not much more for bonds (usually measured by turnover in the secondary market).
- *Outperformance* Over long time horizons, many international markets besides the United States have significantly outperformed the Canadian market, largely as a result of superior economic growth and stronger fundamentals. The Asian meltdown has been unfortunate, but Japan from, say, 1964 to 1989 was an incredibly good ride.
- *Risk reduction* As international markets seldom move in the same direction at the same time (this is termed *negative correlation*), they provide another key benefit of diversification by balancing potential weakness in the domestic market with growth opportunities abroad.
- *Currency hedging* International markets can also provide a useful hedge against any weakness in the value of the Canadian dollar. If the Canadian dollar sinks, the value of international investments correspondingly rises, creating interesting opportunities even with low-yielding, "safe" investments. For instance, given the 8–9% depreciation in the value of the loonie so far in 1998, even a U.S. money market fund returning under 5% looks like a real winner when you tack on the appreciation due to currency weakness.
- *Avoiding foreign content limitations* Even with the higher ceiling for non-Canadian investments in RRSPs (it used to be 10%), it is still only permissible to hold 20% of the book value of a registered plan in international investments. Offshore can be your RRSP equivalent with no foreign content limits.

Of these, portfolio diversification is the major reason for investing internationally. Modern portfolio theory has demonstrated that strategic diversification—spreading investment holdings over a fairly large number of securities by asset class in proportion to the investor's objectives and risk tolerance level—significantly decreases risk, even in the case of volatile assets such as equities. Global investing is the ultimate tool in portfolio diversification, because it substantially augments the range of securities and in some cases even the asset classes available. In addition, as major world markets infrequently move in the same direction by the same magnitude at the same time, investing in nondomestic markets provides an enhanced level of diversification over and above allocation by asset class. For example, academic studies have demonstrated that a strictly Canadian equity portfolio will underperform a mix of Canadian and international investments over the longer term, and with considerably more risk.

Investing in North American and/or global markets through an offshore fund structure provides the double benefits of diversification and offshore protection. And to recap: besides diversification, performance enhancement and risk reduction are two important reasons to invest in nondomestic markets offshore. Since, over long time horizons, many international markets have demonstrated significant outperformance, it is beneficial to be able to access them; this the range of offshore mutual funds can provide. Despite the Asian meltdown, the collapse of Japan or the periodic rise and fall of Latin America, there are still many viable global opportunities to be discovered that are not accessible onshore. And as world markets seldom persist in moving in tandem, they can also reduce portfolio risk by balancing potential weakness in one market with growth opportunities in others. In addition, the currency angle remains key.

It is worth noting that the comparative weakness of the Canadian dollar has been a major contributor to overall returns from global investing in domestic portfolios for some time now. A declining Canadian dollar enhances returns from international investments, which are after all denominated in international currencies, while a rising Canadian dollar has the opposite effect. The impact can be substantial; for instance, global bond fund returns can be highly currency-sensitive. But this is also a double-edged sword. If asset performance is substantially a function of domestic currency weakness, what's going to happen to your global purchasing power if you want to take your investment returns and travel or make purchases abroad? Or in other words, does it make sense to make a strategic investment decision based not on the attractiveness of the investment itself but on the currency kicker effect of a declining dollar? Offshore, this is much less of a problem, since investors can benchmark their holdings to a stable currency other than the Canadian dollar, such as the U.S. dollar, pound sterling, DM or whatever is most convenient. Nonetheless, there is a currency effect whenever investment is two-dimensional (i.e., the stocks or bonds purchased are denominated in a currency other than that of the investor).

Investors concerned about the currency effect have generally had the following options: avoid international markets altogether; actively hedge their foreign currency exposure; or purchase funds with neutral or managed currency exposure. But many investors believe that hedging runs contrary to their longer-term objectives. It's also extremely difficult to call currency movements correctly over any reasonable time horizon, and there are real costs associated with hedging. What's more, there is simply no market to hedge the vast array of minor and volatile currencies where some of the outstanding market returns have been generated. The key point is that for most Canadian investors, owning nonCanadian-dollar-denominated assets is itself a form of hedging.

Pioneering in Offshore Markets

Notwithstanding the comment about many Canadians not being adequately invested in the United States, the U.S. capital markets have traditionally been the first port of call in the development of a global diversification strategy by Canadian investors. But before the development of U.S. and international mutual funds, a haphazard portfolio of a few foreign stocks or bonds was about the extent of most Canadians' global exposure. The growth of U.S. equity mutual funds changed all that by providing investors with professionally managed portfolios that feature active stock selection and reflect the major sectors of the U.S. economy in one convenient and affordable investment. For most Canadians, mutual funds turned the global opportunity into reality.

After the United States, Canadian investors soon began to focus on equity investment opportunities in other major world markets. Then came international money market and fixed-income funds designed to take advantage of the interest rate differential between Canada and foreign markets, and to profit from the currency play that arises as a result. Next on the scene came regional equity funds designed to invest in companies that would benefit from the economic potential of a group of countries that comprise a logical trading or geopolitical bloc, such as the Pacific Rim, Europe or Latin America. The growth of global funds accelerated quickly. It's interesting to note that in 1957, there was one real international mutual fund (the AGF U.S. Growth Fund) in Canada; now, forty years later, there are approximately 400.

Perhaps one name stands out above others in this global investment revolution: Sir John Templeton, founder of the Templeton (now Franklin Templeton) family of mutual funds, and the man *Forbes* magazine described as "the dean of global investing." Starting out from a base in Canada in the 1950s (yes, his funds were originally domiciled in Canada), Sir John has become recognized as one of the most successful investors in history and a legend in his own time. His maxims ring as true today as they did when he wrote or spoke them. Of the many quotes attributed to Sir John, these are some that any aspiring investor should ponder:

- If you buy the same securities as other people, you will have the same results as other people. It is impossible to produce a superior performance unless you do something different from the majority. To buy when others are despondently selling and to sell when others are greedily buying requires the greatest fortitude and pays the greatest reward.
- Bull markets are born on pessimism, grow on skepticism, mature on optimism and die on euphoria. The time of maximum pessimism is the best time to buy, and the time of maximum optimism is the best time to sell.
- To avoid having all your eggs in the wrong basket at the wrong time, every investor should diversify. If you search worldwide, you will find more bargains and better bargains than by studying only one nation. You also gain the safety of diversification.
- *This time is different* are among the most costly words in market history.

Templeton Maxims, 10 Principles for Investment Success

What Sir John first understood years ago was prescient. But today, largely because of the ready availability of market information and information technology, access to global markets is almost universally available. Where a decade ago the levels and performance numbers of foreign markets were of little consequence to North American investors, today they are a focal point of any investment story or telecast. As our technology has expanded, so has our reach for global industry and investment. We reflected earlier that global markets now can react in synchronized movements day in and day out, and that many of the largest international issues trade on a 24-hour basis. While the North American/Western European bull markets of the past eight years have provided some stellar returns and consequently boosted the confidence of many investors, the patina is beginning to show signs of wear. Where do we go from here, and how?

It is important to remember the past in order to make sense of the present and therefore ponder the future. In the 1980s and early 1990s, you couldn't pass a bookstore, read a magazine or watch a financial telecast that didn't mention the coming economic battle between America and Japan. The ever-rising yen and flood of Japanese exports into world markets would undermine and eventually cripple the U.S. economy, so the argument went. Then the Japanese bubble economy burst. Talk of excessive debt, bad loans and financial shenanigans made news and once again the world was safe for America. The problem is, now once more Japan threatens the U.S. economy, this time around via a weak yen, nominal interest rates at close to zero and the possibility of default on government and commercial obligations. Many pundits are suggesting an overhaul for Japan's political and electoral systems and a complete restructuring of its financial system. Solutions are proving difficult to implement and Japan will falter for the foreseeable future before any relief becomes evident; the pace of change in Japan is glacial. But remember: crisis creates opportunity in a world where commerce now transcends borders and currencies, while opportunities exist in the most unlikely places. And companies like Sony, Honda and the like will be around for a while yet.

Alternatively, remember December 19, 1994, when Mexico, to the surprise of just about every investment manager who was overweight with

Mexican bonds and equities, devalued the peso. Mexican interest rates went through the roof, rendering most outstanding bonds worthless, and equities collapsed and inflation exploded. Mexico's citizens faced financial ruin as their ability to repay outstanding loans was now gone, while leading Mexican banks faced possible ruin. Mexico tried to establish a Resolution Trust–style agency to help both the banks and debtors, but events were moving faster than they could react and they desperately needed external help. The government then changed its banking provisions to allow foreign banks to purchase shares in Mexican banks, while Brady bonds were created by consolidating outstanding loans into tradable securities. Meanwhile, many in the industrialized world looked at Mexico's crisis as a prime opportunity to invest, as witness the American, Canadian and European businesses that established manufacturing and assembly plants in Mexico at this time.

There are many such adversity/opportunity stories in the world of international investing. Russia and some Eastern European markets may be the next. But even if individual investors can call global markets correctly, what can they do about it? If you're George Soros or Warren Buffet, you've already established relationships with several leading international investment houses in order to get your pick of global equity and bond issues. Another famous professional investor, Jim Rogers, documents how he went about scouring the world for investment opportunities on a motorcycle in his book *Investment Biker.* Rogers was a cofounder along with Soros of the Quantum Fund and appears regularly on the CNBC Cable Network. *Investment Biker* chronicles Rogers' amazing around-the-world journey. Part adventure story and part economics tutorial, Rogers' advice extends to making investments in exotic countries such as Botswana, Ecuador and the like. Rogers always insisted on buying only the bluest of blue chips such as banks, newspapers and breweries in these countries both as a market proxy and for liquidity. He usually worked through local brokers though he also ran up substantial phone bills to New York as and when appropriate. He also pointed out that investments in these markets do not have to be substantial to eventually yield impressive returns, just selective.

But investment in these economies is not for the uninitiated or faint of heart. So the question offshore investors must ask themselves is: How do you gain prudent international equity exposure and through what means? Even the proliferation over the past decade of global mutual funds can do more harm than good, since the choice can be as daunting as the decision to globally diversify in the first place.

However, if you can't have an account with the Botswana Brokerage Co. Ltd., one of the best sources of offshore fund information is the *Micropal Guide to Offshore Investment Funds* by Robert Milroy. This is an indispensable guide, produced annually, that currently lists, analyzes and ranks in excess of 5,000 offshore funds. Another great source of offshore funds information is the Internet. Many of the best and best-known fund companies have international/offshore funds listings and information online, such as Fidelity Investments, Scudder, Schwab, Vanguard and the like. In other words, many of the U.S. funds not usually available to Canadian residents are available for investment by your offshore advisors. Again, get your money's worth out of your offshore advisor—that's what they're there for.

Exploring the Maze of Global Investment Options

I have never understood why Canadian investors who spend a great deal of time, effort and money to establish an offshore structure so often invest their offshore assets in the same Canadian securities and funds they already hold through their RRSP and/or domestic investment accounts at home. It's true that the task of identifying appropriate global investments can be intimidating. In addition, many investors think that by going offshore in the first place their assets *are* diversified. But if the Canadian equity market corrects, your offshore Canadian equity investments correct, too. You haven't diversified, you have simply doubled your loss potential.

The moral in this, as always, is that any offshore investment portfolio should be a complement to your domestic holdings, offering protection and performance enhancement based on a different set of return expectations. If you are fully invested in equities and fixed income at home, you should consider how to protect your offshore assets through effective diversification by asset class, investment style and possibly currency. The real beauty of the global investment opportunity is your ability to create a portfolio that exhibits a fair degree of what the quants term "negative covariance." In other words, even if the Canadian market tanks, your global portfolio should still be offering you upside potential. In English, that's called intelligent diversification. Also, don't forget that an offshore portfolio must be held in a structure that will best meet your needs, whether it be a trust or a corporate or other structure. The offshore structure is there for your protection, confidentiality and convenience, but it doesn't dictate what you hold in it.

Finally, there is no common denominator approach to offshore, since every solution will be as unique as the individual pursuing a particular outcome. Beginning with a big-picture assessment as part of a disciplined and well researched plan, the smaller, more intricate details necessary to be successful offshore will present themselves as progress is made. The structural components of an offshore plan such as IBCs and other corporate structures as well as trusts are only the shells into which the assets will eventually be placed. Many people make the mistake of falling in love with the form and underestimating the function. This would be the equivalent of admiring the structure of a self-directed RRSP account that was established at a major financial institution which the investor then fails to use to its fullest potential by neglecting to contribute regularly. A waste of time and money.

Dynamics of Offshore Funds

If investors understand the opportunity, access has traditionally been the problem: access to appropriate investment funds and managers whose expertise in global markets will provide an appropriate level of diversification, solid performance and risk control.

There are many variations on the offshore fund structure and the following simply illustrates the most common types of fund currently available. What amazes most investors is the sheer variety of offshore funds available, from straightforward North American equity funds to international and region-specific funds as well as the range of fixed-income funds, mixed funds, laufzeitfonds and specialist funds.

Obviously, investors can also readily hold active portfolios of stocks and bonds offshore, but offshore fund structures provide the same convenience, professional management and liquidity benefits as they do at home while extending your global investment reach far beyond what investors have access to domestically.

Fixed-Interest Stock (Bond) Funds

This is an important sector among offshore funds. After equity funds, fixed-interest funds are more numerous than any other type of offshore fund, with over 1,000 listed in the *Micropal Guide.* The term *fixed interest* covers a wide range of investment instruments, including government, corporate and municipal bonds. Such investments have a relatively low-risk profile, the main risk, of course, being that the bond issuers (the governments or organizations borrowing the money to issue the bonds) will be unable to repay. With stable government issuers, the level of risk is usually acceptable. Because of their lack of creditworthiness, bonds of Third World governments and corporations naturally have more risk. Consequently, the riskier the bond issuer, the higher the yield on its debt. The value of fixed-interest bonds, like that of all bonds, rises and falls in an inverse relationship to their domestic interest rates. It is important to choose a bond fund commensurate with your risk/return expectations. To do that, you must determine what minimum-rated bonds are permitted within the fund, e.g., A or better, AA or better, etc. This information is usually available in each fund's marketing material.

Global Fixed Income

Micropal lists 33 sectors in the fixed-income funds section. Most are single-country funds but there are also global fixed-income, emerging markets fixed-income and other region-specific funds. The largest sector is global fixed-income funds. Offshore investors can gain a diversified mix of fixed-income securities in this sector. This diversification can be advantageous, since selecting the best individual markets can be difficult. Choosing to invest in a number of different global bonds funds is another strategy that can work in an investor's favour: high rates of interest from one fund (riskier) can enhance the yield of a portfolio of low-rate bond funds (less risky).

Laufzeitfonds

Laufzeitfonds are fixed-interest bond funds sold primarily in Germany, Switzerland, Luxembourg and Belgium and may be in differing base currencies. These funds are established with a defined maturity, or collapse date, usually within ten years. When the funds are launched, they usually have a short initial offering period, typically 30 to 90 days, and are then closed to new subscriptions. Thereafter, only a bid price or net asset value (NAV) price is published until maturity. All interest or capital gains are retained within the fund until the end of the fund's life. The fund manager purchases a selection of bonds, in the base currency of the specific Laufzeitfond, with the term of the bonds to be similar to that of the collapse date. Although the manager is not restricted to set maturities for the bond portfolio, it will be liquidated at the term date so that the proceeds will be paid out to the investor. These funds have been very popular in the Luxembourg offshore market, as they are relatively risk-free and attract investors who wish to have funds invested in fixed securities for a set time, with the income generated by the fund being reinvested for the life of the investment period.

Mixed Funds

As the name suggests, mixed funds are invested in a variety of instruments. Since these funds are non-specific in their choice of asset classes, they are very useful to investors who wish to leave the asset allocation decisions to the fund manager. Typically, the manager will attempt to balance riskier equity holdings with fixed-income investments in order to achieve a reasonable rate of return with a relatively low rate of risk. Most of these funds are globally oriented, but often have very different management styles.

Some will have a mix geared to the riskier end of the equity spectrum and/or will also have a higher proportion of equity to fixed income. Others will be more conservative and carry a higher fixed-income/money-market-to-equity weighting. What these types of funds are trying to achieve is often obvious from their names—for example, "managed growth," "balanced" and "defensive."

Money Market Funds

As illustrated earlier, offshore money market funds can differ considerably from what Canadian investors are used to domestically. These debt securities come in various forms. Basically, they invest in securities with maturity dates of less than 365 days, the most common being government issues such as Treasury bills. Other forms of short-term debt instruments are certificates of deposit, bankers' acceptances and commercial paper. Money market funds are the least risky of all offshore funds. Those funds that invest in the securities of stable governments such as U.S. Treasury bills are virtually risk-free. However, money market funds that invest in the treasury issues of smaller countries or commercial paper will take on a little more risk in order to benefit from the yield pickup. Many times, the risk premium is minute compared to the enhanced yield. For example, funds with heavier weightings in private debt or commercial paper run the risk of holding securities that may be in default if the corporation fails. The fund manager may view this risk as worthwhile, since the yield pickup over government treasuries may be greater than the perceived risk. Riskier funds tend to invest in the short-term debt of weaker economies, which have a lower credit rating than traditional U.S. treasuries and short-term paper. The risk of default in these types of funds can be even greater than those invested in the short-term paper of a blue chip company. The *Micropal Guide* has 27 separate categories for offshore money market funds. The majority are single-country funds and most investors would invest in only those funds that are denominated in the currency they use. There are also, however, managed currency money market funds. These are wonderful for individuals as well as institutions who wish to protect the purchasing power of their liquid assets through managed diversification of currency and interest rate exposure. Typically, they invest in a spread of currencies through various forms of short-term paper. The currency positions are monitored on a short- to medium-term basis and the manager looks for undervalued currencies or situations within the currency market that are within the risk/return parameters of the fund. These funds are an important component of global finance, since they are large purchasers of government Treasury bills. Money market funds are a tremendous way to manage liquid assets within a given portfolio; the rates payable will typically be above those paid by banks and other institutions for cash deposits.

Short-Term Bond Funds

Offshore, short-term bond funds are a halfway point between money market and fixed-income funds. While money market funds hold instruments of 12 months or less, fixed-income bond funds hold securities with maturities of more than three years. Short-term bond funds cover the one-to-three-year maturity spectrum. While equity and fixed-income funds are viewed as being a long-term investment, and money market funds are viewed as short-term cash management tools, short-term bond funds fulfill a need in the interim. Not many funds are in this range. Most are invested in German bonds, as they are the most popular, although some Canadian and U.S. short-term bond funds denominated in their respective currencies are available.

Convertible Bond or Debenture Funds

Generally, a convertible bond or debenture is an unsecured loan of a corporation that may be exchanged for ordinary shares in the company, in most cases at the discretion of the bond or debenture holder. As an investment, convertible bond funds tend to work in part like equities and in part like bonds. When the share price of the issuing company rises above the conversion price of the bond, the bond tends to move in line with the price of the underlying shares. But should the share price fall below that of the conversion price, then, as they pay interest and have a limited life, convertible bonds act more like bonds. All this tends to make their performance over time lie somewhere between that of equities and of fixed-interest stocks (bonds). This has great appeal for investors looking for investment growth while being unwilling to take on too much risk. A portfolio of convertible bonds gives an investor a stake in a rising market, while continuing to pay interest regardless of market conditions (so the investor is getting paid to wait). Convertible bonds are not a major area for offshore investment, with only 33 such funds listed in the *Micropal Guide*. The majority of convertible bond funds are invested globally with some area-specific funds, such as those investing in the convertible bonds of Japan, the Far East and Switzerland.

Specialist Equity Funds

Specialist equity funds are at the higher end of the risk spectrum. The *Micropal Guide* splits them into four categories: commodity and natural resource funds, real estate funds, hedge funds and derivative-based funds.

Commodity and natural resource funds obviously invest in the shares of companies operating in sectors such as mining, oil and gas, precious metals, etc. They will also hold physical assets such as gold and other commodities. Real estate funds invest in the shares of companies in property-related industries and/or hold physical real estate, quite often development sites. These hard-asset funds are all too familiar to Canadian investors.

While all these funds feature professional investment management, some fund sponsors take the process one step further by employing a manager-of-managers concept—that is, the services of multiple investment managers are utilized to enable investors to benefit from a range of different investment styles. It's always useful to examine carefully who the sub-advisors are with each fund, if any. Some can really add value, some—well, maybe not.

Derivative funds concentrate on investments utilizing options and futures to achieve high returns. They also include innovative financial technology such as swaps. Futures and other derivative products provide portfolio diversification by enabling investors to participate in many different markets worldwide. Derivatives cover a wide spectrum, from financial instruments, stock indexes and currencies to precious metals, commodities and agricultural products. Used prudently, a well-managed derivatives or futures program can decrease portfolio volatility and improve overall investment returns. Swaps represent an exchange between two counterparties of the total return from a portfolio for a guaranteed income stream over a fixed time horizon. The notional principal—in other words, the portfolio—is not actually swapped; only its dividend or interest income and capital growth are. The principal advantages of swaps include increased returns for the investor with no correspondingly higher levels of risk through greater investment leverage and lower financing costs as a result of implicit economies of scale.

Via derivatives, it is possible to invest in just about all active markets in the world, and investors can enjoy some spectacular returns; but given the leverage and corresponding volatility implicit in these instruments, there is also a major potential for losses. For the sophisticated only!

Hedge funds are similar to derivative funds but with a broader scope. These funds will invest in many areas such as equities, fixed-income bonds or money market instruments, but will also actively speculate in the derivatives market or utilize options and futures as hedging techniques for the underlying securities in the fund portfolio. These funds have gained prominence over the past few years as information on their performance has been disseminated to the investing public, and the risk-adjusted rates of return from some funds have been impressive.

It may not be different this time, but the world of investment opportunities has expanded greatly over the past two decades—not just the global reach of investment opportunities but investments themselves. Hedge funds, which have revisited the prominence they held in the 1970s, are extremely useful tools for investors looking to preserve the integrity of their existing investment portfolios by investing a percentage of their assets in a fund that has fundamentally different investment objectives than their core portfolio. When considering hedge funds, however, longer-term track records are imperative, since the flurry of new hedge funds in the market of late have yet to experience the market conditions they were designed to protect against. In fact, it could be argued that hedge funds have become a bit of a fad, with too many underperforming equity managers leaving major fund companies to start up their own hedge fund (this happened in the 1970s and barely a hedge fund from that era is still in existence).

Another recent development has been the asset securitization fund. These funds usually invest in the uncollected debt of various companies within a given industry or group, such as medical insurance claims from hospitals or outstanding financing for automobile dealerships. Such a fund typically buys a collection or series of outstanding debt payments that are due to be paid by the insurance or other finance companies. This accomplishes two things: the hospital or automobile dealership receives immediate cash flow, at a discount to the actual face value; and that discount, depending on the quality and duration of the outstanding debt, gives the fund an expected rate of return.

These funds are beginning to gain prominence offshore for a number of reasons. They are alternative investment strategies that have proven themselves institutionally in the past and provide a means of diversification from the traditional equity and fixed-income investments that many investors are already overweighted in. The ability of these funds to provide returns depends entirely on the underlying industry and the manager's ability to structure the investment in such a manner as to provide for a continuous stream of maturities—in other words, not investing in a stream of debt instruments that are all from the same carrier and mature at the same time.

The caveat here is the quality of the debt being bought by the fund. The fund should be structured in such a way that the investments being considered by the manager go through a system of checks and balances, preferably by a credible third party, to ensure the quality of the debt instruments. That third party, typically a larger financial institution, should even have the authority to override a manager's decision if the investments chosen do not meet the fund's criteria. These funds, while new to many investors, are an effective means of diversification, again providing a favourable risk-adjusted rate of return.

Research, Research, Research

As Warren Buffet put it, "I'd rather be assured of a good return than hopeful of a great one." The investment world is littered with the broken portfolios of individuals who have spent their investing lives pursuing outperformance. Good or even great returns are only part of the puzzle, and chasing them exposes your investment portfolio to a greater degree of risk than had you invested wisely and left it alone in the first place. A recently published statistic released by Lipper Analytical demonstrates that of 225 U.S. equity fund managers whose benchmark is the S&P 500 Index, fewer than 20% met or beat the index last year. So what? One year is not a very long time and one year does not an investment life make.

The Fidelity Magellan Fund, the same fund made famous by its former manager Peter Lynch, has failed to meet its annual benchmark several times in its history, but who wouldn't want to have owned it for the past 15 years? The problem with the investing public now is that, after nearly eight years of uninterrupted economic growth and concurrently bullish markets, everybody is a genius since most everything people have invested in has borne results in a relatively short period of time. There's an adage in the investment industry: In a bull market you make money and in a bear market you earn it.

With offshore funds, all of the same parameters that are used to determine if an investment is right for your domestic portfolio should be respected. Longer-term performance statistics are more important than annuals, as is the overall investment objective(s) of the fund. Given the above, the age and tenure of the manager(s) of the fund can also be a factor worth considering. Risk/return ratios and volatility indicators are an important component of your decision-making process. You want fund investments for your portfolio that have demonstrated a consistency in their ability to outperform their sector peers and ultimately meet or beat their benchmarks.

One important point worth noting is that offshore funds vary greatly, among themselves and compared to domestic fund investments, when it comes to fees. Many, if not most, offshore funds operate on a front-end-load basis only, with either a range or a fixed amount between 0 and 6% (although there are some funds with fixed front-end loads of 6% and higher). Some fund companies are beginning to offer their investments on a deferred sales charge basis, but this has been limited to only a few companies. Annual fees also vary widely and range between 0 and 3% fixed depending on the type of fund. Switching fees—fees for moving from one fund to another within the same family—range between 0 and 3% as well. Many of the actively managed derivative and actively managed hedge funds have what is commonly termed a performance or incentive fee, paid to the manager when the fund exceeds certain return expectations as indicated in the fund's offering documents (e.g., when the fund exceeds a 10 or 20% annual return). The fee is wide-ranging, usually between 5 and 20% of the total return for the fund.

Fees aside, your motivating factor in making any investment is what I like to call the SWAN ("Sleep well at night") factor. You have to be comfortable as well as confident about the investments you have and the investments you make. If an investment is going to give rise to a higher than normal consumption of Pepto-Bismol or result in many sleepless nights, forgo it. It is better to be invested in funds or asset classes that provide you with comfortable returns and risk parameters that you can live with than invest in the latest "whisper" stock or "rocket fund" that you heard about from your friends and neighbours.

This is why investors must have discipline and patience when tending to their financial well-being. Investors who get caught up in overly bullish enthusiasm at every new high, yet fail to weigh the possibility of a contraction and the effects that may have on them personally, may find the future challenging. These types of investors are typically reacting to what has already happened and are either buying or selling too late and will be the largest casualties when the markets go south. It's not necessarily their fault, but human nature does tend to buy high and sell low.

Fund companies have not been slow to pick up on this. It seems that everybody and his brother is offering a new mutual fund or investment scheme these days. I have been inundated with more offering documents and marketing literature on a veritable hodgepodge of investments over the recent past than I care to remember. From the latest black box solutions for profiting handsomely in the derivatives market to little-known issues in little-known sectors in little-known countries—some of these investments are worth a further look and a little more research, but a great deal more bear serious second thoughts. A rule of thumb: If you don't understand the investment, even after it has been explained it to you, reconsider your participation in it.

If there's a lesson to be drawn from all investment activity, it can perhaps be explained by a piece of word lore. A friend of mine recently imparted this information to me. In Chinese, there is one word that means both crisis and opportunity—and it is spelled and pronounced exactly the same way. This could be the paradigm for the international investor today.

CHAPTER 11

CONCLUSION

The long-term prospects for offshore and international financial, estate and business planning are improving every day. As more and more jurisdictions recognize the need to create a legitimate, efficient and cost-effective environment to attract business and the individuals that own those businesses, the offshore world will certainly expand both in size and in scope. The rise of the individual who no longer views the state as the answer to many of life's problems and ills will continue to confront and confound those in power. Governments in countries like Canada are being faced with issues that were unimaginable ten years ago, such as the accelerated flow of business, money and people to the more efficient locales of the world, or conversely, locales that make doing business with economies like Canada and the United States more efficient and less burdensome. The challenge for countries like Canada in a globalized economy will be in their ability to act and react in much the same way as business, industry, investment and individuals see it, as a much smaller and efficient place than it once was, where money and investments in facilities, machinery, people and locales can be moved at the blink of an eye. The metamorphosis of once-staid old countries with yesterday's ideas of government and finance into leading-edge financial and business centres is happening before our very eyes. Who would have considered Malta, Cypress and Turkey to be efficient (some day) in the areas of global banking and finance? After years of civil war, Lebanon is clawing its way back into the international banking business and the Caribbean and South

Pacific nation states continue to grow in size and scope. While the media, business and governments alike have been hailing the advent of the global economy, very few people have been trumpeting the social and economic changes that are becoming a direct result of globalization, such as the displacement of jobs and industries from one country to another, and the overall effects this may have on a given economy.

While this does not seem fair, it is the way the world now works. Canada's shoe industry of years gone by is now a major employer in Mexico. British Columbia's economic and business future lies south of the border and across the Pacific. Canada's robust resource sector and what is left of our manufacturing sector will continue to face ever-stiffer competition from cost-efficient economies that now have the means, or are quickly acquiring the means, to extract and refine both their natural resources and their people.

Demographics are a double-edged sword that has yet to be fully swung. In all honesty, after the investment boom that will be the result of baby boomer retirement planning, how are nations of geriatric citizens going to meaningfully contribute to slowing economies? This is not solely Canada's problem; it confronts many of the Western industrialized nations. Many of these developments will change the economic and investment landscape of these countries and leave many governments with few alternatives for reducing the debt accumulated during the baby boom years but to raise taxes both directly and indirectly. Western governments need to relieve themselves of their debt, and quickly, in order to be competitive. Whose bonds would you rather own, those of an expanding economy with little debt and a growing GDP or those of a debt-laden society with an aging work force and a shrinking GDP (remember Japan)?

Offshore, it's not just for taxes anymore. In our highly transportable world, business and business solutions will prevail where they can be implemented most efficiently. The challenge for Canadian businesses and business people is determining and finding the means with which they can effectively diversify their businesses to become successful in this globalized world economy as well as put their futures back into their hands. Many of the solutions to these dilemmas can be found in the international world of investment and business. Finding a new and untapped market for products or services that are beginning to lose their appeal in an older economy, effectively diversifying the currency exposure of a business by tapping into a new economy, or simply diversifying as an effective means of expansion—these are all reasons to look to offshore jurisdictions to make these ideas reality.

The first step and perhaps greatest challenge is a shift in thinking. Dropping the border mentality to look for solutions outside the norm is paramount—and, interestingly, not that difficult. Direct investment in industries and businesses in countries that present many of the same variables North America once had has been the tool of investment managers and pioneers for years. Emerging economies have populations whose average ages are typically half that of the Western world, wages are just beginning to show signs of improving, the government is supportive of economic development with minimal intervention, and education and literacy are improving. On top of this is the need for updated and modern means of communications, technology and industrial production and you have what should be considered as opportunities.

Here are some of the indicators to look for. With populations half the age of developed countries, products such as toys, amusements, clothing and food, educational supplies and media items like books, magazines and music will do well. As wages improve many more goods—big-ticket items like televisions, radios and cars—can be bought as well as manufactured in an emerging economy. And the need for improved communications and utilities will rise concurrently. Also with the improvement in wages, more and more children find themselves in school, raising the educational and literacy rate of a new generation of workers. Emerging economies, as well as many of the economies of offshore jurisdictions, are actively looking for direct investment in the areas of light manufacturing, information technology, and hospitality and entertainment industries. Many of these economies are just coming into their own Industrial Revolution, while many more are bypassing the industrial stage of economic development and moving into the information age with the help of companies of the developed world. The PRT Barbados example is a clear indication of what can become of a well thought out plan in an offshore jurisdiction. The extensive list of companies and organizations that can help the entrepreneurial-minded business person plan and implement an international venture ranges from the full-service accounting and consulting firms to lawyers and independent consultants. Enlist their help in carefully assessing your needs and in making the necessary inroads in your new jurisdiction.

For those individuals who are looking to participate in the global economy indirectly, there are a host of service providers who can assist them. Remember, logic, not emotion, should govern the decision-making process in this area. Finding the right advisor(s) offshore usually starts with questioning an onshore expert in the area of international tax and financial planning. You can't venture offshore until your onshore concerns have been addressed. In order to protect your global wealth you will need to diversify into different jurisdictions, asset classes and perhaps currencies. Once the structure or structures that best suit your needs have been established, whether that be a corporation, trust, foundation or a combination of structures, the next step is to determine the investment options available. The world is your oyster at this point, and it will be imperative that the investments you make be commensurate with your risk/return parameters, provide you with effective global as well as sector and asset class diversification, and possibly be tax-efficient. The secret to investment success has always been there: you must be invested, regardless of current market directions, for the long term.

It doesn't end there, as the world of banking and financial services continues to grow in size and scope. The list of services and options available from international financial institutions is growing as well. Services such as internationally accepted debit and credit cards that can be tied directly to a given account are gaining popularity with the travelling set. These cards allow you to access your financial assets from most anywhere in the world, and the balance of the card can be paid directly from its associated cash account with a simple phone call. Also, international brokerage services whereby global securities can be bought and sold through one institution are rising in both prominence and popularity. Offshore venture capital sources and lending facilities, almost unheard of in the past, are another area of expansion. Many of the larger offshore financial institutions with international ties are beginning to broach this area for the international entrepreneur and small business owner/operator.

Where do you find the information you need and whom should you talk to? Before you consider contacting an offshore service provider, you have to sit down and think about what you hope to accomplish. If your only aim is to get your assets out of the country through some elaborate avoidance scheme, never to pay tax on those assets again, so be it. Just be cognizant of the rules and regulations that pertain to resident Canadian taxpayers. There is no shortage of offshore advisors willing to help you do this, and their usual refrain will sound like this: "You are responsible for any and all tax owing on these assets in your jurisdiction. Please sign this form indicating you understand that." If you are looking to establish an international presence with your investment assets and want to conduct your affairs in a planned, diligent manner, you must come to the table armed with a plan. This plan should be open for guidance from your potential advisors. You should also have a series of questions to be answered to your satisfaction before you proceed:

- How long has the company been in operation?
- Who owns the company?
- What is the capitalization of the company?
- What are the assets under administration?
- What does the company specialize in?
- How familiar are the company and its representatives with Canada's tax laws and how they pertain to individual Canadian taxpayers?
- If the company is promoting tax-free solutions, how are they tax-free?
- What structures would they recommend for your plan and why?
- What type of investments or investment management services do they provide or have access to? (This is very important. I have met clients who are invested in products and programs that either they were unfamiliar with or were not suitable to the client's investment parameters.)

- How would the company communicate with clients and the regularity of reporting?
- Ask to see sample statements.
- Ask to see their fee structure and determine whether the fees are inclusive of sundry items such as mailings, faxes, and phone calls.
- Also determine the flexibility of the fee structure.
- Talk to the regulatory bodies in your chosen jurisdiction for information on potential advisors.

Remember these are your assets and your future that you are planning for. Many advisors appreciate organized clients who have at least thought out their plan and have an idea of what it is they want to accomplish, since it makes their work that much easier and enjoyable. An advisor who has answered your questions and provides you with the level of comfort you need should be considered only after you have interviewed a number of others. Be skeptical of advisors who cannot or will not provide you with the information you need to make a decision comfortably. Some have fallen into the trap of placing their business with advisors who have made their services out to be more than what they are. These same advisors, confronted by clients who went offshore to avoid or evade taxes and are now demanding reimbursement or restitution, have said "Too bad. And who are you going to tell?" This puts the clients in an awkward position, since they have in fact gone offshore for all the wrong reasons and fear the revenue authorities more than losing their assets. Let's face it, this has happened onshore plenty of times. That is why you have to be diligent in your planning, implementation and ongoing activities.

As with any offshore planning, the provisions should be carefully reviewed to ensure that they fit the individual's personal family situation. Although there are provisions in the Canadian tax rules allowing for special tax mitigation situations described, many other Canadian tax rules, not specifically intended to apply to these examples, may nevertheless result in the loss of its tax advantages. Specifically, there are a host of technical "traps" that can result in incomplete planning. It is important that all individuals considering offshore planning obtain professional advice so that they are aware of, and are able to take advantage of, these opportunities.

Of all the advantages offshore has to offer, freedom is the greatest. Freedom to plan for your estate, freedom to plan for your future, freedom to plan for your business and freedom to invest anywhere in the world in virtually any asset class. By taking advantage of the myriad opportunities available offshore, you can effectively put the world of business and investment solutions to work for your future, as opposed to depending on others to work for you. A definite offshore advantage.

Notes

1. Press release, Fraser Institute, April 1997.

2. Professor Peter Willoughby, "A comparative approach to tax avoidance and other current tax problems."

3. Press release, Fraser Institute, April 1997.

4. James Dale Davidson and Lord Rees-Mogg, *The Sovereign Individual.*

5, 6. "Can the American workforce grow old gracefully?" *The Economist,* July 24, 1998.

7, 8. Charles Cain, "Introduction to offshore jurisdictions and concepts."

9. Professor Peter Willoughby, "Offshore trusts and companies: a consumer's guide."

10. "The antihero's guide to the new economy," *INC.* Magazine, January 1998; a *CNN/Newstand* telecast on July 22, 1998.

11. Revenue Canada news release, 1997 from www. rc.gc.ca.

12, 13. Revenue Canada Web site and Robert Hindle.

14. Revenue Canada.

15, 16. Garry R. Duncan and Elizabeth J. Peck, *Canadian Residents Abroad*, Revenue Canada.

17, 18. Professor Peter Willoughby, "Offshore trusts and companies: a consumer's guide."

19, 20. Professor Peter Willoughby, "International trusts under fire: the expanding scope of litigation."

21, 22. Professor Peter Willoughby, "Offshore trusts and companies: a consumer's guide."

23, 24. Professor Peter Willoughby, "International trusts under fire: the expanding scope of litigation."

25, 26. Mike H. Azad, Peter G. Fletcher and Hywel L. Jones, *Bahamian Limited Partnerships.*

27–31. Charles Cain, "Company forms."

32. The 4-1-9 Coalition Web site, goldhaven.com, and the U.S. Secret Service Web site.

33. SEC Web site; Yahoo fraud pages; goldhaven.com; International Chamber of Commerce Web site.

34. SEC Web site; Yahoo fraud pages; goldhaven.com.

APPENDIX A

further COMMENTARY AND CASE STUDIES

No investment objective is more important than wealth preservation. While most investors are enjoying once-in-a-lifetime returns in equity markets, financial professionals are now focusing on capital safety. Historically, bull markets tend to end when the public becomes euphoric with the stock market. All indications confirm that we have entered this stage. Alan Greenspan, chairman of the U.S. Federal Reserve Board, made this clear when he recently remarked that the economic cycle has not been repealed. Prudent investors will want to ensure that their recent gains are not threatened by a shift in the market.

Wealth Preservation and Institutionally Leveraged Financial Risks

Since 1997, the financial environment has presented a new and dire range of challenges to those attempting to preserve their wealth. *Those unwilling to examine and confront this situation face the possibility of nothing less than the instantaneous elimination of what was considered safely harboured capital.*

Although wealth has always needed protection from investment risk, it is no longer enough to be protected from inflation, government mismanagement, bouts of deflation or asset confiscation. A new source of risk emerged when the financial services industry introduced derivatives as a regular business activity. Even though investors at large have been given ample warning about the dangers of derivatives trading, an appreciation of the actual risks has not been realized. A review of how the derivatives instrument has affected the economic world in the recent past will illustrate how it is changing the world of banking.

In the United States, the 1980s saw the failure of Continental Illinois. Thereafter, in the mid-1980s the failure of dozens of banks, insurers and savings and loans in Texas, in California and on the East Coast left deep scars upon the U.S. financial system. Today, the pace has quickened and the size of defaults has grown larger. When Confederation Life Insurance Co. was seized by regulators on August 11, 1994, it was the fourth-largest insurance company in Canada, and among the top 30 in North America. In only 60 days it went from AA to bankrupt. With Cdn$19 billion in assets, the collapse of the company eliminated 4,400 jobs. It also threw 250,000 policy owners into disarray in Canada and another 800,000 abroad, to say nothing of the damage to the confidence in Canada's insurance industry.

Then in 1995, came the Barings Bank incident, which turned a venerable and secure institution into a bankrupt one over a weekend. That was the first large bank failure attributed to derivatives. Prior to that event, Procter & Gamble had lost $150 million. For its part, Sumitimo Bank lost in excess of $2 billion in copper-based derivatives trading.

The era of financial engineering and the resulting creation of exotic derivatives have turned secure institutions into speculative ones. On last May 25, *Time* magazine published a review of the North American derivatives market and its potential influence on banks called "The Banks' Nuclear Secrets" by Bernard Baumohl. The article drew an analogy between derivatives trading and nuclear warheads in that there are no small mistakes with either one.

The article cites the U.S. Treasury Department as saying "the 25 American banks with the largest (derivatives) positions have more than $350 billion in credit exposure to derivatives—that is more than enough to wipe out the $250 billion in equity capital that the same banks keep on hand as a cushion to absorb losses. Few believe that Asia's troubles could jeopardize the entire amount—that would take a global, systemic collapse—but the possibility for some big hits is real."

Time succinctly summed up the problem by saying that "the alchemy of derivatives rests on complex mathematical models that predict how markets and derivatives will behave under certain assumptions. The computer models use past market performance to portend the future, but they can't account for the unaccountable: every once in a while an asteroid does strike or countries blow up. These things aren't fully factored in the modeling." U.S. banks have $10 trillion in derivative contracts set to mature this year, and the likelihood of Asian clients reneging on debts may be high. (See the table "Time Bombs?")

Time Bombs?

	Derivatives in Billions Year-End 1997	Credit Risk in Billions Year-End 1997	Risk as a Percentage of Bank's Net Worth
Chase Manhattan	$7,615	$ 82.0	482%
Morgan Guaranty	$6,143	$116.3	1114%
Citibank	$3,024	$ 51.0	297%
Banker's Trust	$2,128	$ 38.5	642%
NationsBank	$1,695	$ 10.4	58%
Bank of America	$1,593	$ 21.8	116%
First National Bank, Chicago	$1,249	$ 12.4	275%
Republic National Bank of NY	$ 271	$ 6.0	183%
Bank of New York	$ 205	$ 2.5	50%
Bank of Boston	$ 146	$ 1.5	34%

Source: Office of the Comptroller of the Currency, Sheshunoff Information Services.

J. P. Morgan, a venerable American bank, is poised to suffer the most from a sudden derivatives crisis. A recent assessment discovered that the bank has a credit risk of upwards of $116 billion from last year. If defaulting creditors renege on even one-tenth of the total amount owing, the bank's equity will be eliminated.

Even large Swiss banks have been caught up in speculating on derivatives. The January 24, 1998 issue of the *Economist* reported that the Union Bank of Switzerland, Switzerland's largest bank, is estimated to have lost US$643 million from Japanese derivative trades that went bad. According to some sources, these losses contributed to UBS having to accept a takeover bid from one of its competitors, Swiss Bank Corp. Fortunately, it is still possible to locate venerable Swiss banks whose derivatives risk is far lower.

Threats to the Canadian Banking System

As the financial crisis in Asia has proven, when a commercial bank reaches a certain corporate size, it exceeds the capacity of regulators and central banks to assist in a crisis. That is the international picture, but it is important to examine whether Canadian banks are better protected.

Annual bank profits in Canada at the moment are huge, but they may not be entirely sound. If the profits are leveraged through large, derivative-linked portfolios, they are at risk. At the last annual meeting of the Canadian Imperial Bank of Commerce, which is extensively involved with Asian derivatives, management consultant Howard Greenspan asked CIBC chairman Al Flood what threat derivative investments posed to the bank. Greenspan was snubbed twice, and never got an answer. Obtaining information about derivatives is difficult, as they are *not required* to appear on a bank's balance sheet. This makes them difficult to assess in terms of risk.

Inevitably, a bear market will replace this bull phase and cause many major banks to be hit a second time. When the present economic stability in Europe and North America subsides and a recession ensues, the effects of derivatives losses will threaten solvent companies. The crux of the problem is the speed of the collapse. If a derivative erupts it does not provide any time to react. Either one is safe before the crisis or not at all.

Richard Thomson, a former merchant banker, wrote in his book *Apocalypse Roulette: The Lethal World of Derivatives* that "derivatives have turned the financial markets into a hi-tech, international 24-hour casino."

He observed that if Asian investors default on derivatives contracts the crash could take only seconds to complete, and would ripple across computer systems around the world.

The reality of world wealth has become more complex than ever before. It is important not only to understand personal investment needs but also to adjust the domicilation of assets in terms of global finance.

On a private client basis, an investor needs to evaluate an institution by asking whether it can:

- Suit specific needs
- Satisfy jurisdictional safety issues
- Provide a corporate style matched to the client
- Ensure that investment performance is risk-adjusted

Unlike traditional measurements based on name recognition, these criteria uncover activities that may not be in the interest of the client. As has been proven, formerly secure banks are now taking unprecedented levels of risk.

The Need for Wealth Preservation Due to the Canadian Dollar and Bear Market

The collapse of local currencies launched Southeast Asia into its depression. Prior to the crisis their currencies were deemed to be fairly valued, since they were anchored by economic growth. The reality of the situation proved to be different than the general expectation.

On July 14, when the Canadian dollar hit another record low, Prime Minister Jean Chrétien shrugged off the loonie's continuing swoon, saying a rock-bottom currency can be a good thing. The July 15 edition of the *Globe and Mail* reported that Mr. Chrétien's comments did not precipitate a selloff on the dollar as had happened previously. Harvinder Kalirai, an economist at Idea Inc. in New York, speculated in the same article that "if that's where Canadian policy is headed, Canadians are going to be poorer in relation to the rest of the world."

The currency of a country is its collective stock. If it is strong it will inspire trust and attract capital. If it is weak it will stimulate export industries temporarily, but diminish the economy in the long run. At a certain point, global currency portfolio managers, hedge fund managers and other speculators will conclude that the currency is weaker than the market believes. At this point, market players will bet against a nation's currency. This cannot be contested, as the markets are always stronger than a nation's central bank.

Consideration 1: The Effect of Changing Demographics on Wealth Distribution

As economies mature, so does the population's mean age. Governments in the developed world can no longer continue to supply the level of welfare provision which, especially over the last 25 years, their citizens have grown used to. The central problem for North America is demographic. An aging population—and the consequent enormous taxes that are needed to support a growing number of retirees—is the most powerful force behind what has become a fiscal nightmare.

Tax Implications As the demographic balance changes in the next millennium, with a higher ratio of elderly people to the population of working age, the cost of this commitment will rise. Since our government pensions are "unfunded" (not matched by a pool of assets), taxes will have to increase. The risk is of a dangerous upward spiral of taxes. Even worse, demographic trends will lead to a drop in the number of people of working age. So if the number of people at work must fall, once more our nation's ability to pay the taxes required to cover the pension burden is undermined.

Since there will be relatively fewer working-age taxpayers, government will have to move gradually from taxation of labour income to taxation of capital income.

Economist David Foot described this in his book *Boom Bust & Echo.* He wrote that in the mid-1990s, large numbers of baby boomers were in their prime earning and spending years. In such a society, a tax system based on income and sales taxes makes sense. *A country with an aging population has to consider increased taxes on interest, dividends, capital gains, and corporate profits. It also has to consider taxes on things that currently are not taxed, including foreign exchange transactions and, in Canada's case, wealth.*

Additional Considerations Further, medical costs for the elderly are much higher than for the young and middle-aged. As the proportion of the elderly in the population rises, the ratio of medical expenditure to national output will increase. With the government responsible for the bulk of medical expenditure, here is another influence certain to drive up tax rates.

Conclusion All this is leading to a recognition that in order to balance their national budgets, governments must introduce stringent cuts in those very services and financial provisions which have previously underpinned their social and political stability. The effect, however, may well be to unleash a phenomenon of social unrest within an emerging dispossessed underclass, which because it has no investment or stake in its society or its future, has nothing to lose from violence, disorder and anarchy, and indeed literally everything to gain. At the same time, the increasingly alienated entrepreneurial elite will be frustrated by the interventions of governments in their wealth creation activities. The share of their profits which governments increasingly demand as a right will put distance between themselves and those whom they increasingly see as a threat, whether they be underclass, radicals or governments.

All planning needs effective forecasting tools. Demographics play a critical role in the nation's economy and social life, and they affect every one of us. The more we understand demographic realities, the better prepared we are to cope with them.

Wealth preservation in the face of issues like these is of paramount importance and investors are exploring many different alternatives.

Consideration 2: Government Disclosure Rules and Money Laundering Issues

Most individuals seeking offshore opportunities are honest, hardworking people. They are innovative and possess a sound sense of judgment, as well as a good dose of common sense. It is important, however, that the prospective offshore investor understand the effect money laundering has had on the banking policies of all major offshore jurisdictions.

It would be impossible to estimate the amount of illicit money laundered throughout the world. Some have speculated the amount to be over US$100 billion per year; others see this figure as a scratch on the surface. In fact, as a result of the rampant money laundering that has taken place in the offshore world, there has been an enormous push to dramatically revolutionize confidentiality and secrecy policies.

Money laundering, and the response to the international nature of the phenomenon, have become leading topics for discussion in both professional and academic circles around the world. The laws reflect the international awareness of the need to strip the profits from criminals as the most potent means of combating international criminal enterprises. Governments earn vote-catching headlines for being observed to be tough on crime, but are these new laws really intended to be used in the way their PR campaigns have threatened? Of great importance is the realization that the new laws are instead being used as a primary means of targeting tax evasion and capital flight mechanisms.

New Legal Dimensions The task of legitimate business is made more difficult by draconian laws which have recently been enacted around the world. In the United States, this task has been further complicated by principles of corporate criminal liability that hold companies responsible for acts perpetrated by low-level employees, often for their own personal benefit and in violation of their employer's policies.

The United States is in the forefront of the development of highly intrusive, extraterritorial legislation that is impacting upon other jurisdictions around the world. The U.S. president signed an Executive Order in October 1995 that identified a number of offshore banking havens as representing a significant threat to U.S. financial interests. It threatened to withdraw U.S. bank clearing facilities from them unless they developed legislation that would allow greater cooperation with U.S. investigations in their jurisdictions.

Today, the mature offshore jurisdictions such as Switzerland, Barbados and Bermuda are developing such legislation. These government directives are imposing a set of statutory rules that must be implemented by all financial institutions:

- Identification information is mandatory in initiating business relationships, individual transactions and business on behalf of another institution.
- Recorded evidence of transactions and the identity of clients must be kept on file for five years after relations with the particular client or group have ceased.
- Internal reporting procedures are mandatory. Every institution must employ a reporting officer.
- Employees of financial institutions must be properly trained in banking procedures and taught to recognize suspicious transactions.
- Organizations are obliged to inform relevant authorities of any evidence that might suggest money laundering.

These directives are quite broad. In addition, in many instances they are in direct conflict with client rights of confidentiality.

The international response to the problem of money laundering has become so intense that the danger now exists that we may be losing our sense of perspective. Governments seem almost obsessive in their quest for more and more information about citizens and investors.

Conclusion The potential investor must give careful consideration to the effect money laundering has had on the offshore banking world. An offshore bank that is negligent in enforcing money laundering safeguards could ultimately put reputable investors' money at risk.

Consideration 3: Canadian Foreign Property Disclosure Rules

General Considerations Currently, Canadians need only report and pay taxes on their worldwide income, but Revenue Canada believes it will be easier to track income or conduct audits if all assets are disclosed.

Accordingly, Revenue Canada introduced new foreign reporting requirements in February 1995, and it became law on April 25, 1997 as Bill C-92. The stated objectives were tax fairness and the elimination of unfair competition by tax evaders. The measures announced included newly expanded reporting requirements for foreign investments and the creation of teams of specialists to handle complex audits of large corporations.

In October 1997, however, the Government announced that it would delay the requirement to report foreign investment property from the first reporting date of April 1998 to April 1999. There is also an examination of alternative mechanisms that may develop more effective measures for the government to achieve its objectives. The trust and foreign affiliate tax reporting requirements announced for 1998 are not included in the new review and are still in effect.

The new rules do not mean more taxes. Taxpayers who are already properly reporting their world income should not be concerned.

Canadian residents are required to report if they:

- Transfer or loan property to a non-resident trust
- Receive a distribution from or are indebted to a non-resident trust
- Own an interest in a foreign affiliate
- Own more than $100,000 of foreign investment property

Disclosure requirements work extremely well in many ways, not necessarily in what they prevent, but in identifying subsequent breaches of the law in the event that something goes wrong, thus providing for a penalty. Put more simply, the British, who have often been the biggest critics of North American regulatory methods, generally assume that those who practise in the financial markets are gentlemen, and they are shocked when

Bank

they discover that their assumptions are often false. The Americans, on the other hand, assume that every person who makes a profit by handling someone else's money has the propensity to be a crook, and they therefore legislate for that possibility.

Is this legislation really aimed at catching international criminals, or are governments merely succeeding in finding new ways to prohibit the international movement of capital?

Protection from Fraud

The time has passed when the individual investor can safely play a hunch with a new and unknown partner, to invest in an institution of which he or she knows little, or to take a risk with an intermediary who promises high returns. Fraud has become the crime of the nineties. It can affect anyone, anytime, anywhere, and it respects no boundaries as it weaves its web of deceit from one country into the next.

Although statistics vary from country to country, one recent study conducted by an international forensic accounting firm estimates that approximately 29% of all fraud is committed against investors, 27% against banks and financial services institutions, 21% against commercial companies, 19% against governments, and 4% in other areas.

Some countries are known to have more than their fair share of resident imposters. Nigeria is one of them, as we saw in an earlier chapter. Law enforcement agencies worldwide are only too familiar with Nigerian fraud. Most often, these criminals are cultured, polished, multilingual, and well educated, and some unscrupulous government officials and business people themselves are often involved.

Although the frauds appear obvious when brought to the attention of international bankers, many astute business people and other individuals are sucked in. Some have been known to fly to Nigeria—at risk, it turns out, to their own lives—to execute business transactions in connection with such a scheme.

There is very little law enforcement agencies can do about it, except caution people about the fraud's prevalence and intricacies. The best way to protect yourself is to become familiar with these operations so that you are not taken in. See the figure for an example of a typical fraud letter.

Sample of a Typical Fraud Letter

Strictly Confidential

Dear Sir:

After due deliberations with my colleagues, I am forwarding this business proposal to you. We need a reliable person to transfer $38.5M into their bank account.

This fund exists as a result of an over-invoicing from a government contract. The contract has been executed and the contractor has been paid. We are now left with the balance of $38.5M that was deliberately over-estimated. As civil servants, we are forbidden to operate or own foreign accounts, therefore we would request that you transact this business, keeping 30 percent of the total for your expenses.

I received your address from our Chamber of Commerce and Industry. I am a top official with the Nigerian National Petroleum Corporation. This transaction is free from all risk.

To get this fund paid into your account, we need to present an international business profile to officials requesting this information. Please forward blank copies of your company's letterhead and invoices, signed and stamped on each page; your banker's full address, telephone, telex and fax numbers; bank account numbers; and private telephone/fax numbers for easy and confidential communications.

You may be required to sign a fund release in our National Bank: three officials will come to your country to arrange this.

Best regards,

Source: The International Banking Security Association

The "Nigerian Model" is bound to be deployed in other jurisdictions and in other forms. *Caveat emptor!* The best investment is always in education; as one philosopher stated, "It pays the best returns."

Emigration Planning

Depressed economic conditions at home, combined with an increasingly global outlook, have Canadians seeking wealth preservation strategies by establishing non-resident status for tax purposes. This usually involves breaking all ties with Canada, and establishing new ties in their chosen jurisdiction.

Planning for individuals who are "multi-jurisdictional" can raise issues of conflicts of laws which can only be resolved through the complex interplay between citizenship, residence, domicile and religion.

Citizenship, Residence, Domicile and Religion

Citizenship or nationality is that right bestowed upon an individual by the laws of the country in which that person was born, or by the laws of the country of which one or both of the child's parents are citizens. Every country has its own rules with respect to whether a child can acquire the citizenship of one or both of its parents, though born on foreign soil. Citizenship is often relevant for the purposes of taxation. For example, all U.S. citizens, regardless of their residence, are subject to U.S. estate and gift taxes on their worldwide income.

Residence is generally determined by the amount of time an individual actually inhabits a jurisdiction and will be a question of mixed law and fact. The Canadian tax system is based on residency, not citizenship. Domicile is also a question of mixed law, but unlike residence a person's domicile depends on the individual's intention. A person can have only a single domicile, but may have a number of residences. The question of residence is one of fact rather than intention.

The importance of particular religious laws, and the effect such laws may have upon estate planning and succession, should be considered in appropriate circumstances. For example, the Sharia law applies to Muslims wherever they reside and may conflict with the relevant laws of their jurisdiction.

Revenue Canada's Interpretation Bulletin IT-221R2 outlines a number of the factors that will be considered in determining whether one will remain a resident of Canada for tax purposes while abroad. These include the permanence and purpose of one's stay, the residential ties retained in Canada, the residential ties established elsewhere, and the regularity and length of the visits to Canada.

Asset Flight and Government Reaction

In response to the fleeing of assets from Canada, the Department of Finance amended laws governing taxation on emigration from Canada. These changes increase Canada's ability to tax, both on the departure of an individual or a trust from Canada and on the disposition of Canadian property by non-residents. It is important that, prior to his or her becoming a non-resident of Canada, all of an individual's assets be examined to determine whether immediate tax is payable or some sort of guarantee must be provided to ensure the tax will be paid. This may be the case whether or not one disposes of assets before leaving Canada.

There are just three countries in the world that levy a departure tax: Australia, Denmark and Canada. Without a doubt, Canada has the strictest emigration rules in the world. In the October 2, 1996 press release issued by the Department of Finance, Finance Minister Paul Martin made the comment that "Canada already has one of the strictest systems in the world when it comes to taxpayer migration. This will make our system even better."

General Principle of Asset Protection Planning

Society is becoming more litigious as the wealth gap between economic classes continues to expand. There is a very real risk that one's lifetime of hard work may vanish due to a vexatious claim that happens to bend the ears of those with the power to decide one's economic fate.

The dilemma is to ensure that defendants who find themselves in legal difficulty do not unfairly deny justice to those they have harmed through fraudulent conveyance of their assets. At the same time, claimants should not have unlimited access to assets used in proper fiscal planning long before they ever became claimants. The exercise is to decide at what point claimants should be disallowed the right to assets placed out of reach by a defendant. Some legal theorists, and an increasing number of offshore jurisdictions, believe that persons who were not claimants or potential claimants at the time of the transfer of assets should not have access to those assets. This is the underlying basis for offshore asset protection planning.

The traditional methods of ensuring that one's financial situation is well protected have become eroded by judgments and legislation that have muddied the wealth-preservation waters. Malpractice insurance may become as difficult to acquire as policies covering directors of Canadian corporations for environmental risks. Courts are scrutinizing transactions to family members, such as placing assets in the name of a spouse (an action that itself carries family law risks). Piercing the corporate armour has also become a favourite court pastime, allowing claimants access to assets in holding companies that happen to be within the court's jurisdiction.

Many common law jurisdictions such as Canada and the United States have adopted the 1571 U.K. legislation known as the *Statute of Elizabeth*, commonly referred to as fraudulent conveyances legislation. Although the intent of this legislation is admirable, in effect it allows claimants to go back in time (even prior to their existence as claimants) to attack transactions which have effectively placed assets outside of the defendant's control. If the claimant is successful, the courts would require the assets to be returned to the defendant where they are then made available to the claimant. The structure of the transaction becomes irrelevant, as long as the assets themselves are within the jurisdiction of the local courts. Should the assets be outside the defendant's jurisdiction, they may still be within the claimant's reach if the courts of the jurisdiction in which the assets are held are willing to enforce a court order from the defendant's jurisdiction.

Creating an arrangement for the pure purpose of protecting assets from creditors would be a conveyance in contravention of most fraudulent conveyance acts. Pursuant to this statute a transfer to defeat, defraud or hinder creditors, existing or future, is subject to attack. However, in many circumstances, offshore arrangements are designed for many purposes and will offer by their very nature some measure of protection from future creditors. Investors may wish to transfer assets outside of Canada because they are concerned about Canada's stability or they fear there will be foreign exchange controls. A client may wish to avoid the *Wills Variation Act* on death by utilizing an offshore arrangement, or may be concerned on marital breakdown about protecting assets for future beneficiaries. Before every federal budget, rumours of an imminent gift tax or limits being placed on the principal residence exemption result in the implementation of offshore strategies.

All of these are legitimate reasons to establish an offshore arrangement, and if the arrangement is a trust or an insurance vehicle the investor is assured some degree of asset protection.

Asset Protection Planning with Offshore Trusts

While a domestic trust will provide a significant degree of protection from one's creditors, an offshore trust can be virtually bulletproof. By introducing an offshore jurisdiction, the settlor introduces a second legal regime, which the creditor must overthrow before gaining access to the trust's assets. To maximize the protection of an offshore trust and the flexibility of moving the trust from jurisdiction to jurisdiction, the assets involved must be liquid in nature. To the extent that an individual is seeking to shield real property located in Canada from potential creditors, an offshore trust is of limited value. However, where cash or securities are involved, the offshore trust can be unassailable.

Other potential benefits of an offshore trust include flexibility of management and control in estate planning situations, the distribution of assets in an unfettered manner (without legislative interference), confidentiality from prying eyes, legal avoidance of estate, succession and wealth taxes and probate fees, and possible income tax savings in certain limited situations. When combined with the asset protection benefits that offshore wealth preservation provides, it is no surprise that professionals are seeking more sophisticated means of achieving their objectives—a path that inevitably leads them to a truly global solution.

A number of offshore jurisdictions have enacted specific laws that modify the undesirable effects of the *Statute of Elizabeth*, while at the same time enabling claimants that have been wronged to access those assets to which they are legally and morally entitled. Each jurisdiction has its own version of these laws and they all have similar core effects. If the claimant can prove in a court of law in the offshore jurisdiction that they have been legally wronged and the assets were transferred subsequent to the wicked action with the defendant's knowledge, the assets are made available to the claimant. Should the claimant fail to prove any of these things, the assets remain as they are (i.e., in the trust for the benefit of the beneficiaries).

Selecting an offshore jurisdiction for the trust enhances the level of protection afforded the trust's property from Canadian creditors. Generally, the courts in an offshore jurisdiction will not provide reciprocal enforcement of a Canadian judgment based upon penal or revenue laws. Whether the offshore jurisdiction will provide reciprocal enforcement of civil awards will depend upon principles of comity among nations, or upon specific reciprocal enforcement conventions.

Hence, the claimant must prove his or her case in the courts of the offshore country. However, this applies to civil claims only, and matters involving criminal activity will normally entail cooperation with the jurisdiction that is seeking the return of assets.

Guidelines for Creating an Offshore Trust

1. Appoint only trustees that are non-residents of Canada and residents of the desired jurisdiction for the residence of the trust.
2. Make sure the location of the trust's assets is outside of Canada and in the desired jurisdiction for the residence of the trust.
3. Make sure that no person other than the trustee is exercising a substantial portion of management and control over the trust unless that person is a resident

in the jurisdiction in which the trust is intended to reside. The following are examples of persons, other than trustees, who may be found to be controlling the trust:

a. A protector or another person given supervisory authority over the trustees and the trust. Even if the protector only has the power to appoint and remove trustees and no powers to control or limit the disposition of trust assets, it is possible that the protector might be found to be controlling the trust by the threat of removing a trustee who does not follow his or her instructions and replacing him or her with a trustee who will. It would be different if the protector had the power to appoint new trustees only if existing trustees resigned.
b. An investment advisor who operates on a discretionary basis. If the investment advisor makes investments without being required to first seek the approval of the trustees, he or she may be found to be controlling the trust.
c. A settlor who attaches to the trust document a memorandum or letter of wishes requesting but not compelling the trustees to follow certain instructions in administering and disposing of the trust assets. If the trustees closely adhere to the memorandum, it may be found that the settlor is effectively controlling the trust.

Another interesting aspect of an asset protection trust is that the creditor protection automatically extends to the beneficiaries of the trust. Since the trustees will likely have discretion with respect to the timing and amounts of payments to the beneficiaries (i.e., a discretionary trust), they can simply withhold payments from beneficiaries that have become bankrupt, insolvent or indebted to creditors, until such situation is rectified.

Although the trust is a very flexible and convenient vehicle for holding assets in several situations, the asset protection aspect is limited not by the trust structure itself, but by the jurisdiction in which the trust is located. Transfer of property to the trust can be attacked in a fashion similar to that for the transfer of property to any individual. It is this aspect that the offshore jurisdictions have specifically addressed in their local legislation. Transfers to trusts can be conveyed back to the transferor only under very specific circumstances. As mentioned earlier, if the claimant can prove in a court of law in the offshore jurisdiction that he or she has been legally wronged and that the assets were transferred after this wrongful claim arose and with the defendant's knowledge, the assets will be ordered reconveyed to the transferor. In many of the offshore jurisdictions, an intent to defraud must also be proven by the claimant, and a statute of limitations usually exists (two years in the Bahamas; six years in the Cayman Islands). However, even if the claimant is successful, the trust remains intact, and only the amount necessary to satisfy the proven claim will be ordered reconveyed.

The offshore asset protection legislation attempts to bring into balance the rights of both the settlor, who may want to provide for the future welfare of his or her family and descendants, and any creditors or claimants who have a legitimate right to assets that have been improperly placed outside their reach.

Asset Protection Planning with Insurance Companies

A review of Switzerland's insurance company law reveals that the Swiss legislature has imposed upon the Swiss insurance industry probably the most rigorous asset management regulations and investment limitations imposed by any nation.

One may not have a need for supplementary life insurance coverage; however, when appropriate, the acceptance of a modest supplementary amount of insurance coverage can provide international investors with unique capital preservation provisions.

As an example, a single-premium endowment is a one-time, single-deposit investment made through an insurance contract from which a very small insurance premium is deducted. This deduction contractually provides for a supplementary death benefit payment. It is due to this "insurance policy feature" that some of the most unique benefits exist, which are not accessible anywhere else.

The basic contractual agreement for the single-premium endowment can be set for an "intended" 5-, 10-, 15- or even 20-year duration. Most importantly, investors may cancel their contracts at any time before the expiration of any such period and recover all of the accumulated cash value including dividends and interest.

If a person residing outside of Switzerland purchases a life insurance policy from a Swiss insurance company and designates his or her spouse or descendants as beneficiaries of such insurance policy or irrevocably designates any other third party as beneficiary, this insurance policy is protected by Swiss law against any collection procedures instituted by the creditors of the insured person and is also not included in a Swiss bankruptcy procedure. Even if a foreign judgment or court order expressly orders the seizure of such policy or the inclusion in the estate in bankruptcy, such an insurance policy may not be seized in Switzerland or included in the estate in bankruptcy. Creditors may seize the policy or have it included in the estate in bankruptcy only if the purchase of the insurance policy or the designation of the beneficiaries is considered to be a fraudulent conveyance under Swiss law. This condition is fulfilled if the insured person purchased the policy or designated the beneficiaries less than six months before the bankruptcy decree was issued or the assets seized in a collection procedure. It is also fulfilled if the insurance policy was purchased or the beneficiary designated with the clear intent to damage creditors. This intent, however, cannot be proven if the life insurance is purchased and the beneficiaries are designated at a time when the insured person is solvent and no creditors have asserted any claims against the insured which could result in insolvency.

If the insured person has designated a spouse or descendants as beneficiaries of the insurance policy, it is protected from creditors irrespective of whether the designation is revocable or irrevocable.

Investors seeking capital transfer privacy, the long-term safety of a sound currency, the best protection available against the risk of future exchange controls, historically proven protection against creditor lawsuits and a secure and flexible capital depository will find the structure of a single-premium endowment worthy of review. Others who prefer a more investment-focused instrument should review the benefits of a Swiss annuity certificate.

How to Pick the Appropriate Bank

The dilemma facing many professionals responsible for sourcing offshore financial facilities is the choice between the one-stop-shop banks, which promise to be jacks of all trades, and the boutique banks, which are masters of one. Here is our guide to selecting the appropriate financial institution.

The overwhelming majority of investors do not yet fully appreciate the inherent safety limitations contained in the credit ratings issued by most ratings agencies. This constitutes a severe danger. Due to the analytical methodology they've adopted, most ratings agencies are forced to rely on business data that is at least three to six months old. Reliance on such delayed data renders the eventual credit ratings and safety evaluations of dubious quality when a crisis erupts. Witness the Asian crisis, when ratings agencies failed to alert investors and depositors in a timely fashion.

On a private-client basis, an investor needs to evaluate an institution by asking whether it can:

1. Suit specific needs
2. Provide a corporate style matched to the client
3. Ensure that investment performance is risk-adjusted

Unlike traditional measurements based on name recognition, these criteria uncover activities that may not be in the interests of the client. As has been proven, large banks are now taking unprecedented levels of risk.

How to Pick the Appropriate Trustee

The trustee must be a bona fide trustee, licensed, regulated and insured in the jurisdiction in which they reside. Insurance and regulation are important features, as the trustee is accountable for the preservation of the assets and must act in the best interests of the trust. Trustees are accountable for negligent acts and clearly have a fiduciary duty to the trust.

A point often forgotten is that the basic definition of a trust depends on the high degree of confidence that must exist between the settlor and his or her trustee. The personal trustee is inevitably subject to illness or death and can at times be tempted to disappear with trust assets. While a corporate trustee may not die, similar liability issues may exist and indeed be exacerbated by the fact that a corporate trustee enjoys limited liability. Moreover, in some instances, settlors and beneficiaries are not in a position to make legal claims against trustees. For this reason, extreme care must be taken by the settlor in choosing a trustee, who must be in a position to demonstrate not only longevity and capability, but also a financial strength that would permit that trustee to have deep enough pockets to cover the potential liabilities incurred by employees.

The Global Insurance Industry

As stated earlier, a review of Switzerland's insurance company laws reveals that Swiss legislators have imposed upon the Swiss insurance industry probably the most rigorous asset management regulations and investment limitations imposed by any nation. Like many financial analysts, we believe that Swiss insurance companies are the safest on earth. As such, the insurance industry sections of this guide will focus exclusively on the Swiss insurance industry. The conclusions contained within result from the same methods employed to analyze global banks. Additionally, appropriate emphasis will be used to highlight certain specific realities, which do not apply or are not found in other segments of the Swiss financial industry.

For each franc Swiss insurers promise to pay, they must have at least one franc in asset. That prudence is still a "world exclusive" and it is very good indeed.

Supervision is governed by the Swiss Federal Bureau of Insurance. It is the Bureau that sets the general investment guidelines and regulations, as well as monitors the industry's investments, spot-checks at frequent intervals the holdings and balance sheet valuations of these companies, and at times demands the liquidation of investments deemed to be inappropriate to the general investment portfolio. It is the same Bureau that supervises the general asset allocation decisions and enforces the rules, which specify that only an infinitely small percentage of the company's assets may be invested outside Switzerland, or in the Swiss stock market. Specifically, Swiss insurance companies are not allowed by Swiss law to invest at large in non-Swiss bonds. They may only purchase Swiss government, cantonal, bank or AAA corporate Swiss bonds of Swiss borrowers for 95% of their bond portfolio. Only 5% may be invested in high-quality foreign bonds.

After weighing all known factors that compose the Swiss insurance industry's basic safety potential, it is hard not to conclude it is a provider of some of the most secure investment alternatives in today's financial world. Still, not all Swiss insurers offer equal safety. Some are more exposed to derivative risks. Others are part of a consortium with corporate assets exposed to U.S. or Canadian regulators, creating a distinct repatriation risk. One such Swiss insurer was recently ordered to stop accepting new U.S. clients because the parent ownership was very active on U.S. soil and did not want to suffer risk of corporate asset seizure. Still others employ custodian banks, which are heavily involved in derivatives, creating a custodial risk to the Swiss insurer. All relevant facts must be considered when selecting an insurance provider.

Example of Offshore Insurance-Linked Wealth Preservation Programs

The ultimate wealth preservation, investment-oriented paper-denominated instrument means:

- A certificate guaranteed by the absolutely safest investment instruments in the world
- Complete investment liquidity and flexibility
- Attaining the highest possible net returns on the very safest paper issued by the best credit-rated governments
- Full Swiss creditor protection against legal claims (including governments)
- Certain Canadian investors may avoid the foreign reporting requirements as drafted by Revenue Canada

- The option to participate in professional currency management by Europe's leading currency/investment management houses at an institutional-level discounted fee

These services are available exclusively through a properly tailored Swiss Annuity Certificate offered by a distinctively wealth preservation–oriented insurer.

Canadian Tax Planning and Offshore Structures

As described, the primary objective in the establishment of an asset protection structure is to put assets beyond the reach of creditors in a tax-neutral fashion. In the case of a trust, provided that it is properly structured, this objective can generally be met.

To the extent that the trust is designed to blanket a tax plan, the settlor will want to attempt to achieve some form of tax benefit such as the tax-free growth of the assets of the trust. To the extent that the trust earns passive investment income, this latter objective is very difficult to achieve. But there are several exceptions.

The taxation in Canada of the income of an offshore trust is governed by section 94 of the *Income Tax Act.* Generally, the rules in section 94 operate to deem a discretionary non-resident trust to be a trust resident in Canada, provided that certain preconditions are met; and deem a non-discretionary non-resident trust to be a controlled foreign affiliate so as to be subject to the Foreign Accrual Property Income (FAPI) rules. The applicable tests are very complex and very broad. Any planning undertaken to circumvent the application of these rules may well be subject to the general anti-avoidance rule in subsection 245(1) of the Act.

In assessing how or when to consider the use of offshore trusts from a Canadian perspective, a number of questions should be asked at the outset:

1. Where does the individual reside?
2. Of what country is the individual a citizen, particularly if the country of citizenship taxes on the basis of citizenship and not residency such as the United States?
3. Who are the beneficiaries of the individual's will and of what countries are those persons residents or citizens?
4. What is the nature of the property or activity the individual wishes to deal with, where is it located, and if it is within Canada, can it be moved offshore?
5. Who owns the assets that will be transferred into the offshore trust structure? How long have those assets been held by the individual? What is the tax cost, and for how many years has the owner been resident in Canada, if at all?
6. If the person who will settle the trust was resident in Canada but has ceased to be a resident of Canada, how long ago did that status change?
7. Is the individual, if a Canadian resident, anticipating a gift, bequest or inheritance from someone not a resident of Canada?

Subsection 94(1) of the *Income Tax Act* sets out two basic tests, the beneficiary test and the contribution test, to determine whether an offshore trust is deemed a Canadian resident for tax purposes.

1. *Beneficiary test.* The beneficiary test is cast in broad terms. Subsection 248(25) of the Act speaks of a person "beneficially interested in a trust." A person is considered to be beneficially interested in a particular trust if the person has any right as a beneficiary under the trust to receive, whether directly or indirectly, any of its income or capital. The right may be immediate or future, absolute, contingent, conditional on or subject to the exercise of any discretionary power by any person. Simply put, the test is satisfied where at any time in the taxation year a person beneficially interested in the trust is:
   a. Resident in Canada
   b. A corporation or trust (either resident or not resident in Canada) with which a person resident in Canada was dealing not at arm's length

or

   c. a controlled foreign affiliate of a resident in Canada

2. *Contribution test.* The contribution test has two parts:
   a. The source of the trust's property, which is concerned with the source from which the trust directly acquires its property

and

   b. The source of the trust's interest, which is concerned with indirect acquisitions of trust's interests

Subparagraph 94(1) (b) (I) of the Act states that the "contribution test" is satisfied where the non-resident trust acquires property directly or indirectly in or before the taxation year of a trust from a person who:

1. Has acquired property from the trust, in any matter whatever from a beneficiary or relative as defined by subsection 2521(2) of the Act

and

2. Was a resident of Canada within the 18-month period before the year-end of the trust's relevant taxation year

and

3. Has been a resident in Canada for more than 60 months or is from a trust or corporation not dealing at arm's length

The above requirements are cumulative and must all be satisfied in order for section 94 of the Act to apply.

The "contribution test" is also satisfied where the beneficiary acquires any or all interest in the trust directly or indirectly by way of:

1. Purchase
2. Gift, bequest or inheritance from a related person

or

3. The exercise of the power of appointment of a related person

Recent Draft Legislation on Certain Offshore Trust Situations

In addition to the Canadian Foreign Property Disclosure Rules described earlier, in December 1997 the Department of Finance released draft legislation affecting offshore trusts. Unlike the foreign reporting requirements, the proposed amendments to the definition of "beneficially interested" may cause certain trusts to become subject to Canadian tax that have not been in the past.

The definition of "beneficially interested" is proposed to be expanded to include a person not beneficially interested at the particular time, and:

1. Because of the terms or conditions of the trust or any arrangement in respect of the trust at the time, the person might, because of the exercise of any discretion by any person, become beneficially interested in the trust at the particular time or at a later time

and

2. At or before the particular time, the trust has acquired property from such person, or a person not dealt with at arm's length

These amendments raise the concern that any non-resident trust with a Canadian-resident settlor/contributor that is not within the permitted five-year exemption period may be subject to tax in Canada, notwithstanding the fact that it does not have any Canadian-resident beneficiaries, so long as it permits the addition or substitution of beneficiaries.

For instance, Revenue Canada could take the position that where there is a Canadian-resident settlor/contributor to an offshore trust which permits the addition or substitution of beneficiaries, this situation could now be considered even if the trust document precludes Canadian-resident beneficiaries. This is because a Canadian resident could become a beneficiary if he or she ceased to be resident in Canada, and so he or she is beneficially interested in the trust.

This draft legislation, if enacted as is, would likely rule out some outbound trust strategies described below, especially the more aggressive ones that were set up with the intention of changing beneficiaries at a later date.

Examples of Tax-Efficient Offshore Structures

Tax-Efficient Inbound/Outbound Planning

These types of trusts are also known by other names such as "granny trusts" or "inheritance trusts." Simply put, if an individual resident in one jurisdiction leaves assets for the benefit of an individual resident in another jurisdiction, it may be possible for the income earned by that gift or bequest to accumulate in an offshore trust free of Canadian income tax.

Immigrant Trusts

As we have mentioned a few times, Canada taxes individuals on the basis of residency rather than citizenship. On becoming a Canadian resident—a status that depends on a number of factors—an individual will be subject to Canadian taxes in respect of his or her worldwide income at the applicable Canadian rates. These rates vary depending on the amount of taxable income, the type of income and the province of residence. Passive income of non-Canadian corporations or trusts in which the immigrant has the requisite interest will also be taxed directly in his or her hands on a yearly accrual basis.

There is a special provision in Canada's tax rules which allows up to a 60-month grace period for income earned by a certain type of offshore trust, even if the trust is funded by an intending immigrant. These trusts are commonly known as *Canadian immigrant trusts* (CIT).

A CIT is a discretionary trust established in a tax haven by an individual who is considering becoming, or has recently become, a resident of Canada. While there are a variety of structures for CITs, depending on who the beneficiaries are, generally speaking CITs provide that:

1. The persons given the power to deal with the property (the "trustees") have full discretion as to the payment of income and capital to the persons entitled to share in the trust property and the income earned on that property (the "beneficiaries").

2. The CIT cannot be resident in Canada and the trustees cannot be controlled in any way by Canadian residents.

A CIT allows an individual to earn investment income and capital gains for a period of up to five years without paying Canadian tax. As well, with proper planning the Canadian tax cost of the property held by the trust can be increased by any appreciation in the value of the property that occurs during that period, with the result that no Canadian tax will be payable on accrued gains on the eventual sale of the property.

While the period of the tax exemption is commonly referred to as being five years, the actual period ends on January 1 of the year in which the immigrant has been resident in Canada for a total of 60 months. For example, if an individual became a resident of Canada in December 1993, the period would end on January 1, 1998. This illustrates the importance of timing the move to Canada. If the individual had instead become a resident of Canada in January 1994, the period would have ended on January 1, 1999 (i.e., by delaying the move for one month the tax exemption period would be extended for an additional year).

Active Business Planning: Planning for the Canadian Entrepreneur

Barbados is a unique jurisdiction that combines the benefits of an offshore safe haven with a network of taxation treaties. With a foreign affiliate international business company (IBC) set up in Barbados, Canadian corporations can carry on international operations such as marketing efforts, exploration, resource development or any number of other functions. The income generated from these operations is taxed in Barbados at a top rate of 2.5% (scaling down depending on the amount of revenue). This money can be repatriated to the Canadian parent in the form of dividends. Careful planning must be done to ensure that corporations and their affiliates are properly positioned to benefit from this structure, but the rewards are obvious—an extremely tax-efficient way to tap into international markets.

The Offshore Asset Freeze: Planning for the Canadian Entrepreneur

Many businesses held in the form of private corporations aspire to grow. However, once that growth is achieved, the owners find that huge capital gains have accrued—on which taxes will eventually have to be paid. Proper planning at the initial stages of a company's growth can save taxes not only from ongoing dividend payments, but potentially large amounts in the event of the sale of the corporation. Furthermore, efficient tax and estate planning with respect to the owners' personal situations may be achieved simultaneously with the business plan.

The primary reason for an asset freeze is to cap taxes in a growth situation. If a company worth $1 million is on the verge of taking off, the common shares can be recalled and replaced with preferred shares at the fair market value of $1 million. A structure subscribes to a new issue of common shares that will rise in value as the company expands.

As part of deciding whether to complete an asset freeze, one must review one's estate planning and business objectives. This exercise should include examination of the assets, liabilities, revenues and expenses of today, and the estimation of future amounts and requirements. The decision to freeze must be made with this financial information. For example, should one implement a freeze if access to some or all of the expected future growth may be required?

Typically, dividends from the private company will be taxed at an effective rate of 39% in the hands of the owners/taxpayers. Once these dividends are put to work in the form of investments, the second-generation income will attract further tax in the hands of the taxpayer. With an asset freeze, however, dividends will be paid to a Specialized Resident Business Corporation in Barbados which holds the common shares on which the dividend payments are made. This results in a withholding tax of 15% on these dividends paid in Canada, and no tax on the dividends because of the special status of the company in Barbados. Furthermore, the income will then flow to an offshore trust, and unlike a domestic freeze in Canada, the investment income will not attract any second-generation tax due to the international trust legislation in Barbados.

Currently in Canada, the capital growth in certain private Canadian company shares can accrue tax-free to the shareholder to a maximum lifetime limit of $500,000. However, 75% of the increase in share value over this limit will be taxed in the hands of the shareholder at personal income tax rates should the shares be sold or transferred. The estate freeze in effect transfers this growth element to the Barbados structure. The Canada-Barbados tax treaty allows for the sale of the shares held in the structure to be free from capital gains tax. Barbados itself does not tax capital gains accrued by such a structure. The exceptional rate of growth of many companies may lead to huge tax savings for the owners in the event of the sale or transfer of the company.

In addition to minimizing income and capital gains taxes, the asset freeze may also have the advantage of:

- Providing for succession of the business
- Protection of assets from litigation
- Protection of assets against spousal claims on marital breakdown (self or beneficiaries)
- Privacy
- Greater investment alternatives
- Diversification from all assets being potentially governed by one court
- Diversification outside of Canada

In special situations, all the fees (consulting, inception, annual and legal) for the structure are absorbed by a *venture capital corporation* in exchange for a small percentage of the common shares. This would be a small cost to pay relative to the potential capital gains tax due in Canada.

The Business Case for Going Offshore

"In retrospect," Jack Jones thought, "I should have done it years ago." Given the advantages his company now derives from its international business company set up in the Bahamas, the rationale for going offshore is clear. It wasn't always that way.

Discussions that Jack had with his colleagues about going offshore often centred on the very real attractions of asset protection and tax planning. However, having first-hand experience, Jack found that one of the greatest advantages of setting up offshore is the ease and convenience of business administration. In many offshore jurisdictions, no taxes of any kind are imposed on the income or assets of international business companies. In addition, there is often far less government regulation to comply with and even fewer reporting requirements. For this reason, many companies that carry on business internationally have found that basing their international operations in an offshore jurisdiction can reduce operating costs significantly.

The Company

Jack Jones is the president of Tool & Dye Ltd., a Canadian distributor of machine parts. Tool & Dye orders parts on behalf of its Canadian customers from several suppliers in Europe. The company then delivers these parts to its various customers throughout Canada. After several years of growth in the early 1990s, Tool & Dye Ltd. had developed a significant customer base in the United States. To better serve its U.S. customers, the company incorporated a subsidiary in the United States. The parts that Tool & Dye Ltd. imported from its European suppliers would then be reshipped to the American subsidiary.

The fortunate turn of events for Jack came in 1994 when, through a series of business contacts, he was asked to assist in setting up an in-house maintenance operation offshore for a colleague's company. After several business trips for this purpose, Jack began to realize how much easier it was for his colleague's offshore company to carry out its distribution activities.

Jack consulted with his most trustworthy friends and obtained professional advice on the concept of setting up his own international business company in the Bahamas. Tool & Dye's offshore operation was set up in an efficient and cost-effective manner in 1996. At present, the operation has accomplished two important purposes. First, the offshore company entered into a joint venture agreement with a local machine parts distributor that served to provide the company with its first international business customer. Second, and perhaps more importantly for Jack, he was able to arrange his own business affairs and reap several tax benefits.

The Incentives

Through the concept of reinvoicing, Tool & Dye was able to purchase the parts needed for its Canadian and American customers through the international business company. The latter now resells these parts directly to Tool & Dye Ltd. in Canada or its American subsidiary, and retains a reasonable portion of the profit tax-free in the Bahamas. This structure has already allowed Jack to increase his capital much more quickly, and consequently to benefit from the availability of more capital in order to grow his international business.

Additionally, Jack was able to solve a major foreign exchange problem. When all purchasing was made by Tool & Dye in Canada, the latter would pay for the purchases in U.S. currency but would invoice its Canadian customers in Canadian currency. Often, this money management would cause a serious loss on the value of exchange between the Canadian and American currencies. This problem is still particularly prevalent today.

A similar challenge would also apply, from time to time, on the intracompany sales from Tool & Dye to its U.S. subsidiary. With the addition of an offshore company, Tool & Dye still continues to suffer foreign exchange losses, but the losses are now trapped and paid to the international business company instead of the various banks which provided the U.S. dollars to Tool & Dye. Consequently, what was once a major expense item before taxes for the company has now been neutralized.

The business of Tool & Dye Ltd., its subsidiary in the United States and the international business company still runs along the very same lines as when Tool & Dye was founded. The big difference, however, is that by integrating the advantages offered by an offshore jurisdiction, the business has very legitimately reorganized some of its financial and administrative elements and its profitability has increased appreciably.

Personal Advantages

As usual in these cases, the non-business advantages were also very attractive to Jack. The opportunities in tax and estate planning, on a personal level, which opened up as a result of his entry into the offshore world have enabled this Canadian businessman to situate himself and his family in a position which offers many more very legitimate alternatives in terms of accruing, enjoying and disposing of personal assets.

International Business Planning with FAPI Rules

With the increased globalization of business during the past decade, Canadians have become more interested in and aware of the opportunity to legally structure their international business affairs in order to take advantage of various provisions of both Canadian income tax law and the corporate and business law of various other countries, commonly referred to as "tax havens." The provisions of our tax legislation known as the FAPI rules (see above) may be particularly suited to international business planning.

The general principle of FAPI requires that Canadian taxpayers report, and pay tax on, their worldwide income. However, exceptions to this general rule do exist. One that is particularly pertinent may be found in part of section 95(1)(b) of the *Income Tax Act* of Canada:

> (b) "Foreign accrual property income".—"foreign accrual property income" of a foreign affiliate of a taxpayer, for any taxation year of the affiliate, means the amount, if any, by which the aggregate of: (I) the affiliate's income for the year from property and businesses *other than active business.* ...[emphasis added]

There are, most certainly, other relevant areas of law, both income tax and otherwise, which should be consulted and considered when formulating plans and structures for international business matters. However, many areas of international business in which Canadians participate may benefit from consideration of the potential application of the FAPI rules.

A case which is typically appropriate for the creation of an offshore international company is that of three partners in the software licensing business, residents of Canada, the United States and Great Britain respectively. In this case, each of the partners owns software licensing rights which they had independently marketed in their own jurisdictions. Their joining together was prompted by the business decision to create a more marketable product internationally from the synergy which the partners felt would result from the combination of their products. Where and how to do it, though, was the issue.

In order to avoid business and legal problems for each of them, it was decided that the international business should be centred in an independent jurisdiction. To accommodate this business goal, an offshore tax jurisdiction was the logical choice. First, none of the partners had previously conducted any international sales. In fact, there had never even been any attempt at marketing the products internationally. Therefore, any assets to be transferred to the offshore company would currently be of nominal value. Second, it was decided that the international company would immediately reassign, to each of the partners in their own jurisdiction, the exclusive rights for that jurisdiction. In this way, it was clear from the beginning that no attempt was being made to avoid declaration of revenue or imposition of taxes on the respective businesses already in operation.

The joint venture structure was arranged such that the Canadian, an individual, would own 40% of the international company. Additionally, the Canadian would wholly own the British company and the latter would hold 20% of the international company. The American, an already established corporation, would hold 40%. The licensing rights for international sales would be transferred by each of the partners to the offshore company in exchange for a percentage of future royalties. The offshore company would then market the licensing rights internationally and receive the royalties from such future sales. In this way, the sales revenue would attract no taxation in the offshore venue, the principal purpose being to allow the new international company to accumulate capital much more rapidly than if the revenue were brought into the jurisdiction of any of the three partners where it would be immediately taxed.

The consequence, therefore, of the foregoing may be that, if properly structured in accordance with the relevant provisions of income tax law applicable in Canada, the portion of the net income earned by the international company which would otherwise be attributable to the Canadian taxpayer will be exempt therefrom, due to the fact that it would very likely, under Canadian income tax laws and regulations, constitute active business income in the hands of the international company.

However, when considering joining with foreign partners for the purpose of constituting an offshore corporation, one should bear in mind that the tax treatment given to controlled foreign affiliates may not be the same in other jurisdictions as in Canada.

In the United States, it would appear that the passive income of a foreign affiliate is generally included pro rata in the income of its U.S. shareholders. However, certain income derived from active business may also be included if the affiliate falls under the purview of Subpart F of the *Internal Revenue Code.* Subpart F income comprises, among other things, "foreign base company income," which may include revenues from various sources such as rent, shipping, the sale of goods or services to related persons, etc. Unless the case could be established whereby the particular royalty revenue resulting from the operations fell clearly into one of the specifically exempted categories of foreign income, the U.S. resident would likely be assessed and pay tax on its proportionate share of the international company's annual revenues.

Likewise, in the United Kingdom, tax laws may apply to a controlled foreign affiliate if it is subject, in its country of residence, to a lower level of taxation on its profits for a similar accounting period. In addition to meeting this requirement, a foreign affiliate must be the object of a specific direction by the Board of Inland Revenue in order to be subject to U.K. tax laws. British shareholders of such an affiliate may have to include in their income a share of its profits, unless the affiliate qualifies under one of various statutory exemptions, such as the pursuit of certain defined activities.

The two brief commentaries above on possible applications to U.S. and U.K. taxpayers, however, are nothing more than observations on potential applications of income tax laws in those jurisdictions. It is important to note that no one ought to rely upon opinions on legal matters in these two jurisdictions unless they are furnished by a legal practitioner duly authorized in that particular jurisdiction.

Nonetheless, the added advantages of security to the business assets from foreign claims and the simplicity of business operations favour the establishment of the international business company's operations in the foreign jurisdiction.

Consequently, the proposed structure may, subject to other legal and accounting requirements, offer certain elements of synergy to the partners (particularly, the Canadian). The foregoing could provide a long-term, possibly even permanent, tax holiday to the international business company in its business operations in the offshore jurisdiction, to which may be added an indefinite deferral of tax consequences to the Canadian majority partner. This serves to furnish the principal benefit of allowing the international company to accumulate and retain capital, for business expansion and other purposes, at a much quicker rate than if the partners continue to operate their own individual businesses from their home jurisdiction. Additionally, the lack of corporate and administrative law constraints in the international jurisdiction allows the partners to concentrate on the effective and fluid management of the business in a very progressive manner.

While it must always be borne in mind that the foregoing scenario is likely not completely and directly analogous to any other particular set of business circumstances in which the reader may actually, or plan to, be involved in, the increasing trend toward doing business internationally may still benefit from the general principles of this case. Naturally, no one should rely on the principles of this case without extensively consulting their own legal and financial consultants.

APPENDIX B

RESOURCE GUIDE

Unlike many other offshore publications, the following resource guide is not a compendium of every offshore bank, lawyer, advisor or company in every offshore jurisdiction in the world. It contains contacts in the various areas of offshore in several jurisdictions that I have had the pleasure of knowing and in many cases conducting business with. As a private client it is not necessary for you to match up all the necessary relationships (i.e., which bank with which legal firm with which trust or investment company?)—many of the service providers listed below have a series of strategic relationships to effect the necessary steps in order for you to become successful offshore. This guide is merely to help you begin the process of finding the relationship that is right for you. It also contains information on other offshore publications and sources of additional information such as Web sites.

Banking

comprehensive banking services

Bank of Ireland (Jersey) Limited

P.O. Box 416, Bank of Ireland House, Francis Street
St. Helier, Jersey JE2 4QE — Tel. 01534-59959
Channel Islands — Fax 01534-37916

Mr. Joe O'Leary
Managing Director

The Royal Bank of Scotland (Nassau) Limited

P.O. Box N-3045
3rd Floor, Bahamas Financial Centre
Shirley and Charlotte Streets
Nassau, NP — Tel. (242) 322-4643
Bahamas — Fax (242) 326-7559

Mr. Matt McNeily

Coutts (Bahamas) Limited

West Bay Street
P.O. Box N-7788
Nassau, NP — Tel. (242) 326-0404
Bahamas — Fax (242) 326-6709

Mr. William K. Thomson
Private Banking

Trust Services

Thorand Trust & Management Limited
IDB House, East Bay Street
P.O. Box N-3242
Nassau, NP
Bahamas
Tel. (242) 393-8622
Fax (242) 393-3772

Mr. Robert Lotmore
President

Matheson Trust Company (Jersey) Limited
P.O. Box 316
Jardine House
1 Wesley Street
St. Helier, Jersey
Channel Islands JE4 8UD
Tel. (44) 1 534 888111
Fax (44) 1 534 888118

Mr. Alan V. Tidy
Managing Director

Royal Bank of Canada Trust Company (Bahamas) Limited
P.O. Box N-3024
Nassau, NP
Bahamas
Tel. (242) 322-4980
Fax (242) 323-3407

Mr. Paul Patterson
Managing Director

St. Vincent Trust Services Limited

European Office
Stadtle 7
POB 70
FL-9490 Tel. 41 75 236 1433
Vaduz, Liechtenstein Fax 41 75 233 2593

Caribbean Office
Trust House
112 Bonadie Street
POB 613 Tel. (809) 457-1145
Kingstown, St. Vincent W.I. Fax (809) 457-1961

Leadenhall Trust Company Limited
P.O. Box N-1965
Nassau, NP Tel. (242) 325-5508
Bahamas Fax (242) 328-7030

Mr. David Rounce

BNP Private Bank & Trust Bahamas Ltd.
Beaumont House, 3rd Floor
Bay Street
P.O. Box N-4883
Nassau, NP Tel. (242) 326-5935
Bahamas Fax (242) 326-5871

Attn: Client Relations Department

Investment Services

including investment management, brokerage and insurance-based investments

Britannia Consulting Group
3rd Floor
Tradewinds Building
P.O. Box CB-12724
Nassau, NP
Bahamas

Tel. (242) 326-5205
Fax (242) 326-5349

Mr. Hywel Jones
President

Dominion Investments Ltd.
P.O. Box SS-6827
Bahamas Financial Centre
Nassau, NP
Bahamas

Tel. (242) 326-4528
Fax (242) 326-4721

Mr. Martin Tremblay, C.A.
President

Equity Management Group Ltd.
Bahamas Financial Centre
P.O. Box N-3716
Nassau, NP
Bahamas

Tel. (242) 356-9229
Fax (242) 356-9234

Mr. Jeff Robinson

International Portfolio Analytics Ltd.

3rd Floor
Norfolk House
P.O. Box CB-12407
Nassau, NP
Bahamas

Tel. (242) 356-7371
Fax (242) 356-7375

Mr. Anthony Ferguson, CFA
President

RBC Dominion Securities (Global) Limited

Saffrey Square Suite 103A
Bank Lane
P.O. Box N-1063
Nassau, NP
Bahamas

Tel. (242) 328-0077
Fax (242) 328-0079

Mr. Kevin Kelly

RBC Dominion Securities (Global) Limited

Cardinal Plaza
P.O. Box 1095GT
Georgetown, Grand Cayman
Cayman Islands BWI

Tel. (345) 949-4066
Fax (345) 949-0092

Mr. John Bond

Cayman National Securities Ltd.

Cayman National Building
P.O. Box 275GT
Grand Cayman
Cayman Islands BWI

Tel. (345) 949-7722
Fax (345) 949-8203

Mr. Dan Martiuk
President

Skandia

Skandia AFS Bahamas Ltd.
Saffrey Square, Suite 102
Bank Lane
Nassau, NP
Bahamas

Tel. (242) 356-9450
Fax (242) 356-9452

Ulrika Hedrok
Senior Representative

Altamira Financial Services (Barbados) Inc.

International Trading Centre
Warrens, St. Michael
Barbados, West Indies

Tel. (246) 425-4940
Fax (246) 425-4944

Mr. Kieran Young
Private Banker

Comprehensive Services

company formations, company management, fund administration, planning and individual services

Skye Fiduciary Services Limited

Skye Suite
Molfort House
2 Water Street
Ramsey
Isle of Man
IM8 1JP
British Isles

Tel. 01624 816117
Fax 01624 816645

Mr. Charles A. Cain
Executive Chairman

Globacor Consultants Corporation

Private Wealth Preservation
BCE Place
Bay-Wellington Tower
181 Bay Street
Suite 2810
Toronto, Ontario
M5J 2T3

Tel. (416) 410-8082
Fax (416) 207-9502
E-mail globacor@consultant.com

BDO Dunwoody

Chartered Accountants
Royal Bank Plaza
P.O. Box 32 — Tel. (416) 865-0200
Toronto, Ontario M5J 2J8 — Fax (416) 865-0887

Mr. Garry R. Duncan
Tax Partner

Cardinal International Corporation Ltd.

3rd Floor
Norfolk House
Fredrick Street
P.O. Box CB-12618
Nassau, NP — Tel. (242) 356-6326
Bahamas — Fax (242) 356-6328

Mr. Stephen Hancock, FCA
Director

Ms. Wendy Warren
Director

International Company Services (Gibraltar) Limited*

Suite 2B
Mansion House
142 Main Street — Tel. Gibraltar 76173
Gibraltar — Fax Gibraltar 70158

Mr. Francis Whiteland
Consultant

*Offices in: Isle of Man, London, Portugal, Turks & Caicos, Dublin and Hong Kong.

Price Waterhouse Coopers

Gardner House
Wilton Place
Dublin 2, Ireland

Tel. 353-1-678 9999
Fax 353-1-662 6616

Mr. Peter O'Dwyer
Director
Financial Services
E-mail: peter.odwyer@ie.pwcglobal.com

KPMG Peat Marwick

Chartered Accountants
P.O. Box N-123
Nassau, NP
Bahamas

Tel. (242) 322-8551
Fax (242) 326-5622

Mr. Gregory P. Cleare
Partner

Price Waterhouse Coopers

Chartered Accountants
Providence House
P.O. Box N-596
Nassau, NP
Bahamas

Tel. (242) 322-8543
Fax (242) 326-7308

Mr. Thomas Hackett
Partner

The Winterbotham Trust Company Limited

Bolam House
King & George Streets
P.O. Box CB-13253
Nassau, NP
Bahamas

Tel. (242) 356-5454
Fax (242) 356-9432

Mr. Brent Haines
General Manager

The Winterbotham Trust Company (Uruguay) S.A.

P.O. Box 12.128
Blanes Viale 5910
11.500 Montevideo
Uruguay

Tel. (598-2) 61 65 44
Fax (598-2) 61 76 14

Ms. Carmen Forcella
General Manager

Legal

Prof. Peter Willoughby
The Old Mill House
St. Ann
Alderney — Tel. 44 1481 823925
Channel Islands — Fax 44 1481 823228

Prof. Peter Willoughby, Consultant

Deacons Graham & James
3rd–6th Floor
Alexandra House
Central — Tel. (852) 2825 9211
Hong Kong — Fax (852) 2810 0431

Lennox Paton
Counsel and Attorneys-at-Law
P.O. Box N-4875
Devonshire House
Queen Street
Nassau, NP — Tel. (242) 328-0563
Bahamas — Fax (242) 328-0566

Mr. Michael L. Paton
Partner

Byers Casgrain
Barristers & Solicitors
1 Place Ville Marie
Suite 3900
Montreal, Quebec
H3B 4M7

Tel. (514) 878-8800
Fax (514) 866-2241

Mr. Constantine A. Kyres
Partner

Hess Devries Menorak
405—1167 Kensington Cres. N.W.
Calgary, Alberta
T2N 1X7

Tel. (403) 299-9177
Fax (403) 299-9172

Mr. Richard W. DeVries, B.Comm, LL.B.
Barrister & Solicitor

Hindle & Associates
1350 Sherbrooke Street West
Suite 1420
Montreal, Quebec
H3G 1J1

Tel. (514) 843-8929
Fax (514) 843-4872

Mr. Robert Hindle, B.A., B.Comm., B.C.L., L.L.B., F.R.I.

Mr. William Johnston, LL.L., LL.B.
9 Barton Street
Ottawa, Ontario
K1S 5M6

Tel. (613) 730-8000
Fax (613) 730-0143

McKinney Bancroft & Hughes
Mareva House
4 George Street
P.O. Box N- 3937
Nassau, NP
Bahamas

Tel. (242) 322-4195
Fax (242) 328-2520
E-mail mcbanhu@bahamas.net.bs

Ms. Meta McMillan Hughes
Partner

Kleinfeld & Giacosa L.L.P.
Suntrust International Center
Suite 1940
One S.E. Third Ave.
Miami, Florida
33131

Tel. (305) 892-1000
Fax (305) 358-6541

Mr. Denis A. Kleinfeld
Principal

Publications

offshore magazines, periodicals and books

Magazines

Offshore Finance Canada

Canada's only magazine of offshore and international tax, business and investment subjects written specifically for the Canadian market. Published six times per year.

OFC Publications Inc.
2 cours des Fougères
Nun's Island, Quebec
H3E 1X6

Tel. (514) 769-2805
Fax (514) 769-4252
e-mail. island@aei.com

Mr. Brian Stammer
Publisher

Offshore Investment

The venerable offshore magazine out of the U.K. Has regular contributions and editorials from some of the best minds in the industry.

Published by:
European Magazine Services Ltd.
62 Brompton Road
Knightsbridge
London
United Kingdom
SW3 1B1

Tel. 44 171 225 0550
Fax 44 171 584 1093
Web site. www.offshoreinvestment.com/offshore

Mr. Barry C. Bingham
Publisher

Offshore Outlook

Known for regular in-depth features of various offshore jurisdictions as well as topics.

Published by:
Ginsglobe Communications Inc.
1510 Cantera Avenue
Santa Barbara, California
93110

Tel. (805) 682-6318
Fax (805) 563-9528
e-mail. Ginsglobe@earthlink.net
Web site. www.offshore-outlook.com

Mr. Johan A Wassenaar
Chairman

Shore to Shore
Magazine.

Published by:
Highbury House Communications PLC
The Publishing House
1-3 Highbury Station Road
Islington, London N1 1SE
United Kingdom

Tel. 44 171 226 2222
Fax 44 171 704 1021

Mr. Barry Engel
Editor

International High Flyer
Upscale *Robb Report*–type magazine aimed at the offshore marketplace.

Published by:
Division One Travel Media
The Publishing House
1-3 Highbury Station Road
Islington, London N1 1SE
United Kingdom

Tel. 44 171 226 2222
Fax 44 171 704 0752

Mr. Sean Cronin
Editor

Books*

The Micropal Guide to Offshore Investment Funds

An indispensable guide of over 5,500 funds, including a survey of the top-performing funds as well as other rankings and important information. Edited by Robert B. Milroy.

Published by:
International Offshore Publications Limited
Box 549
Les Sablons, St. Peters
Guernsey, Channel Islands
GY1 6HS

Tel. 44 1481 66759
Fax 44 1481 66758
E-mail info@intl-offshore.com
Web site www.intl-offshore.com
U.S. & Canada sales 1-888-848-8844 (toll free)

* For other books and publications see the list of Web sites on the following pages.

Web Sites

Mondaq Business Briefing
www.mondaq.com
This site, indispensable for anyone attempting to conduct international business, covers many more issues than just offshore. It is a very large and tremendous source of business, legal and regulatory information, and includes a global directory and database of international financial and legal professionals.

Goldhaven.com: Your Offshore Information and Tax Haven News Source
www.goldhaven.com
This Web site will be of particular interest to anyone who is searching for information and books concerning offshore. It features a book review section to assist in choosing the right book and also has a new release and pending release sections. There are also links to newsletters and other information sources.

The Fraser Institute
www.fraserinstitute.ca/
A decidedly alternative view of what the media provides as to the state of affairs in Canada. The Institute publishes regular updates and press releases on subjects such as the tax, finance, business and economics of Canada.

Escape Artist
www.escapeartist.com
While I don't necessarily agree with the name of this site, it is a good source of references to country and regional service providers, including banks, investment managers and other service providers, broken down by jurisdiction. The site has a decidedly American slant, but it is still a great source of information. The reference sections will be of interest to all who love information, since they include everything from weather and real estate to currencies, embassies and job opportunities. A fun site.

The International Chamber of Commerce

www.iccwbo.org

A source of global commercial issues. The representative body that speaks on behalf of enterprises from every sector around the world. The site is also an important source of information on scams and fraudulent activities such as the "prime bank instruments" scam, and there is an entire book on the subject available from ICC publications.

Nigeria: The 419 Coalition Web Site

www.home.rica.net/alphae/419coal/

An offbeat yet useful site describing the Nigerian scam in detail and providing additional information on fighting the scam, and listing contacts for additional information and reporting from sites such as the U.S. Secret Service. The site also contains samples of the faxes and letters used to perpetrate this scam.

Revenue Canada

www.ic.gc.ca

What book about offshore could be considered complete without reference to the revenue authority? Take the time to peruse this vast site carefully—the sheer amount of information will make you reconsider your on-line plan for the amount of time that can be spent here. Just for fun, under "Search" type the keywords "underground economy" and read some of the dozen or so releases—then try to tell me it's not time to consider a change in emphasis from direct taxation to indirect taxation.

Index

Complete Your Offshore Library

Vol 2 No 1
January/February 1997

Vol 2 No 2
March/April 1997

Vol 2 No 3
May/June 1997

Vol 2 No 4
July/August 1997

Vol 2 No 5
September/October 1997

Vol 2 No 6
November/December 1997

Vol 3 No 1
January/February 1998

Vol 3 No 2
March/April 1998

Vol 3 No 3
May/June 1998

Vol 3 No 4
July/August 1998

Are you missing any issues of *Offshore Finance Canada*? If so, why not order back copies to complete your library.

Act fast while supplies last

To order, call today!
(514) 939-2800

Please allow 3 to 4 weeks for delivery.
Fax: (514) 939-2881; Email: island@aei.ca

In Canada, each issue is CDN$20.00 or six issues for CDN$75.00
In the United States, each issue is US$15.00 or six issues for US$78.00
Outside of North America, US rates plus US$3.00 each for S&H